294.
343
MOR

LOOKING INTO WORLD RELIGIONS

BEING A BUDDHIST

PEGGY MORGAN

B.T. BATSFORD LTD   LONDON

CONTENTS

3	Introduction	33	Celebrating Festivals
4	Buddhist Sources	35	Giving Generously
6	Being a Buddhist	38	Giving Loving Kindness and Friendship
8	Hearing the Dharma and Waking Up	41	Being a Part of the World
10	Taking Refuge	44	Developing Compassion
12	Making Offerings to the Buddha	47	Giving Everything you have
14	Following the Path	50	Going on a Pilgrimage
17	Taking the Precepts	53	Accepting Death
20	Choosing the Right Livelihood	56	Cremating and Remembering
23	Being in a Family	59	Entering into Nirvana
26	Meditating	62	Difficult Words
29	Joining the Sangha	64	Index

Front cover: (top) A Burmese child uses a large bell to make a musical offering to the Buddha, at Shwe Dagon pagoda in Rangoon (courtesy Kate Poole); (bottom left) Buddhist monks, their faces expressing the qualities of friendliness, compassion and loving kindness (courtesy the Buddhist Society); (bottom right) this Buddhist shrine in the Chinese city of Canton is as simple and modest as the Shwe Dagon pagoda is complex and elaborate (courtesy Robert Harding Picture Library).

Frontispiece:
All of us need a teacher – someone who is wiser than we are – to help us to master the basic tools and skills that we need in order to read religious texts and understand them for ourselves. A Buddhist teacher is also a spiritual friend. Traditionally it is monks who have the care of the dharma and the task of passing it on to future generations.

ACKNOWLEDGMENTS
The Author and Publishers would like to thank the following for permission to reproduce copyright illustrations: Barnaby's Picture Library, pages 11, 14, 49, 54 and the frontispiece; the Buddhist Society, pages 7, 8, 36, 38, 42 (and front cover); the Camera Press; pages 19, 26, 45 and 56; the Ceylon (Sri Lanka) Tourist Board, pages 33 and 51; Zena Flax, page 29; Anne-Marie Gaston, page 23; the Idemitzu Art Gallery, Tokyo, page 59; Roger Jones, page 21; the Mandel Archive, page 13.

© Text and selection Peggy Morgan 1989

First published 1989

All rights reserved. No part of this publication may be reproduced, in any form or by any means, without permission from the Publisher.

Typeset by Tek-Art Ltd, West Wickham, Kent
Printed in Great Britain by
Courier International,
Tiptree, Essex
for the publishers
B.T. Batsford Ltd,
4 Fitzhardinge Street, London W1H 0AH

ISBN 0 7134 6015 6

INTRODUCTION

People have been following the teachings of Gautama Buddha for over 2500 years all over the world, from India where he lived, to Europe and America, where Buddhism is growing rapidly today. The Buddha claimed to have found an ancient noble path which leads from suffering to a state of peace and happiness called Nirvana. Because Buddhists believe in an ultimate reality, Buddhism is a *religion*. Buddhists do not, however, call this reality a personal God. This means that some people, including some Buddhists, prefer to call Buddhism a *philosophy of life* rather than a religion. Perhaps more important than either of these terms, is the emphasis on following a path, and that Buddhism is a *way of life*, not just a set of abstract ideas.

There are many levels involved in being a Buddhist. Those born into a Buddhist family absorb the ethical ideals and practices as they grow up. They hope to live within these ideals all their lives as generous and honest lay people. They believe that good moral actions bring a better rebirth in a future life and that through many such births they may make steady progress towards Nirvana.

Some Buddhists, however, decide to become world-renouncers, that is, monks or nuns. These *bhikshus* and *bhikshunis* are respected in Buddhist culture as being closer to the state of enlightenment than ordinary householders (lay people), although Buddhists never say that householders cannot be enlightened and there are examples in all forms of Buddhism of their attaining the highest state.

Just as there are different levels at which people can be practising Buddhists, so there are different types of Buddhism. Most Buddhists (though not all) consider these different schools of Buddhism as different forms of practice and outlooks which suit the different temperaments of people rather than being right or wrong in themselves. The main types of Buddhism are the Theravada which is found in Sri Lanka, Thailand, Burma, and other parts of South-East Asia as well as in the west. Mahayana Buddhism, which is found in China, Korea, Japan, and Tibet and the west. Mahayana Buddhism contains many other schools within it, such as the Pure Land, Zen and Tibetan (Vajrayana) Buddhism.

This book considers what being a Buddhist means. It tries to emphasize both activities and experiences, which is why the title of each section includes an "-ing word". Religious practice always involves a movement from external actions to the inner transformation of the heart and mind. Some of the sections in this book deal with the external actions, and some with the emotions and spiritual sensations of believers.

Buddhists teach that what is written down needs to be interpreted by people practising the religion. The sources quoted in this book will take you only so far – you will need to meet as many different Buddhists as possible and find out from them what being a Buddhist means.

BUDDHIST SOURCES

The quotations in this book come from many different sources. These represent the wide variety of texts and styles of teaching that are part of the long history of the Buddhist religious tradition which is more a family of traditions than a single entity. The sources quoted in this book are a reflection of the Buddhist tradition as a whole and show the wide range of different attitudes of Buddhists to their sources. Each section contains three sets of quotations in it.

* Many of the quotations in the first set are taken from the *Pali Canon* which is respected to a greater or lesser degree by all the schools of Buddhism; but I have also included material from other sources in this first set. Some of these are from commentaries or by writers that are important in the Mahayana traditions. One such quotation is even from a modern source, because Zen Buddhists have always qualified their use of scriptures, maintaining that the living authority of the *dharma* is "outside the scriptures".

* Some of the *sutras* which are particularly important in the Mahayana schools are included in the second set of quotations. Examples of these are the *Vimalakirti Sutra*, the *Lotus Sutra*, and the *Diamond Sutra* which is part of the *Prajnaparamita* literature. Although they are included in the second set, these quotations are from the primary sources of doctrine and teaching for Mahayana Buddhists, who believe that these *sutras* are as much "Buddha word" as the *Pali Canon* is for Theravadins. Some of the sections contain almost entirely Mahayana material in all three sets of quotations.

* The third set is drawn from all parts of the Buddhist tradition. The Theravada quotations come from both traditional and modern western sources. There are also extracts from the Pure Land, from Tibetan and Zen traditions and from a new western movement called The Western Buddhist Order. Quotations from other new movements, such as the many Nichiren groups are not included because of lack of space and not because they are not considered as part of the Buddhist tradition.

COLLECTIONS OF TEACHINGS

THERAVADA Buddhists believe that shortly after the death of Gautama Buddha there was a council at Rajagriha. At that council, senior members of the monastic *sangha* listened to and checked a recitation of the rules for the *sangha*'s life (the *vinaya*), and the sayings of the Buddha (the *sutras*). It was then passed on orally from monk to monk for many hundreds of years. Later councils checked the accuracy of the collections and a third section of material called the *abhidharma* (higher teachings) was added. These collections were translated into Sanskrit and the local Indian dialects used for teaching Buddhism. They were also later translated into Chinese and Tibetan and included in the Mahayana collections of scriptures described below.

Buddhism was taken to Sri Lanka in the third century BCE in the reign of the Indian Emperor Ashoka. The three oral collections of teachings were brought to Sri Lanka in the Indian dialect called Pali. In the first century BCE they were written down on long thin strips of dried palm leaf. The palm leaves were collected in three (*tri*) baskets (*pitaka*). This collection of Pali texts made in Sri Lanka is called both the *Tripitaka* and the *Pali Canon*. The three sections are the *Vinaya Pitaka*, the *Sutra Pitaka* and the *Abhidharma Pitaka*. Theravada Buddhists believe that these scriptures provide the accurate word of Gautama Buddha which determines the way of life and beliefs of Buddhists.

The MAHAYANA schools do not reject the *Pali Canon*, and they have their own version of much of the material in it, written in Sanskrit or Chinese. They also have other *sutras* which they claim as authoritative and believe are also "Buddha word". Some of the most famous Mahayana *sutras* quoted in the text of this book are listed below. They are very difficult to date accurately but seem to have emerged sometime between the second century BCE and the second century CE.

The *Vimalakirti Sutra* is about a remarkable white-robed layman, Vimalakirti, who is able to lead an enlightened life while fully immersed in the world. In this way he hopes to help others towards enlightenment, using *upaya kausalya* or "skilful means" – a common theme in Mahayana *sutras*.

The *Prajnaparamita Sutras* are a collection of Mahayana *sutras* which teach a wisdom (*prajna*) which goes beyond (*paramita*) conventional understanding. One of these is the *Astasahasrika*. This title means "eight thousand lines", but there are also expressions of this material in *sutras* of 18,000, 25,000 and 100,000 lines. Sometimes the teaching is distilled into very short texts, such as the *Vajracchedika* or *Diamond Sutra*, and *Hridaya* or *Heart Sutra* which are quoted later in this book. The aim of the *sutras* is to help people to understand that the underlying nature of everything is the nature of enlightenment.

The title of the *Saddharmapundarika Sutra* can be translated literally as the "True Law Lotus" and it is particularly famous in Chinese and Japanese Buddhism. It explains that all the different Buddhist paths are merely parts of the one path to Nirvana. It was used by the sixth century CE T'ient'ai school in China (which became the Tendai school in Japan in the ninth century) to harmonize existing teachings. The thirteenth-century reform groups under Nichiren also focused on this *sutra* and it remains important to the Nichiren new religious movements.

Sukhavati Sutras are named after the Buddha land or realm of Amitabha. Sukhavati is usually translated as "pure land" but "land of happiness-having" is a more literal title. These *sutras* are used by the Pure Land schools who believe that saying the name of Amitabha Buddha with faith, or with faith and good works, will lead to rebirth in the Pure Land. Once a devotee is with Amitabha, his skill in helping others by his teaching is so great that they will soon attain Nirvana.

There are two main groups of canonical collections or *sutras* made by Mahayana Buddhists. One is the Chinese collection which is called the *San Tsang* or *Three Storehouses*. This collection is the result of 12 centuries of translation work which began in the first century CE.

The second collection was made in Tibet in the fourteenth century CE. This collection was called the *Kangyur* or "translated word" of the Buddha. A separate collection called the *Tangyur* contained hymns, commentaries and works on logic and medicine. The collections are linked with the scholar Bu-ston, or Buton.

CONTINUING TEACHING

Buddhists do not think of the teachings of the Buddha, or the "Buddha word" as what is past and unchanging. There have always been respected commentators and teachers to unpick and interpret the texts for each new generation. And so the sources of the Buddhist tradition continue to grow.

BEING A BUDDHIST

In one way being a Buddhist means belonging to a particular community of people and following a path of life taught by the Buddhas (enlightened beings) in particular Gautama Buddha, the Buddha for our age. (He is also sometimes called Siddhartha or Shakyamuni.) Belonging to this community means being a member of the Buddhist family. Members of the Buddhist family make up a fourfold assembly or *sangha* with male and female householders (lay people) and world-renouncers (*bhikshus* and *bhikshunis*). However, according to the Buddhist tradition there is a more important aspect of Buddhism than being part of an institution. The Buddha is said to have taught two things: suffering and the end of suffering. He also pointed out that seeing and following the teaching (*dharma*) was seeing and following him. This *dharma* is the truth about the way things are. The *Dharmapada* summarizes it in the following words:

> Not to do any evil, to cultivate good, to purify one's mind, this is the teaching [*dharma*] of the Buddhas.

Being a Buddhist involves understanding and following this teaching and doing so to help all living beings from their state of suffering in *samsara* (the round of continued birth and rebirth) to a state of everlasting joy and happiness called Nirvana. Being a Buddhist means putting aside any sense of separateness between oneself and others by purifying the heart of greed, hatred and ignorance. It is then possible to share with others the states of loving kindness, compassion, sympathetic joy and equanimity which are at the heart of Buddhism.

MOVING INTO THE TRUTH

A wheel (*chakra*) was one of the attributes or qualities of a universal ruler or great king in ancient India. It symbolized his richness, authority and command. Many of these attributes are also given to the Buddhas. Gautama Buddha's first sermon, part of which is quoted below, is often called "setting in motion the wheel of the law". Law here translates the word *dharma*. His authority is not a matter of issuing commands: he helps to awaken people to the truth about the way things are, so that they can test this truth out by their own experience.

In this sermon from the *Pali Canon* many basic Buddhist ideas are introduced, such as the Four Noble Truths, the Noble Eightfold Path, the need to be selfless and the transitory nature of the world. Buddha said:

> "The spokes of the wheel are the rules of pure conduct; justice is the uniformity of their length; wisdom is the tyre; modesty and thoughtfulness are the hub in which the immovable axle of truth is fixed.
>
> "He who recognises the existence of suffering, its cause, its remedy, and its cessation has fathomed the four noble truths. He will walk in the right path.
>
> "Right views will be the torch to light his way. Right aims will be his guide. Right words will be his dwelling-place on the road. His gait will be straight, for it is right behavior. His refreshments will be the right way of earning his livelihood. Right efforts will be his steps: right thoughts his breath; and peace will follow in his footprints."
>
> "Whatsoever is originated will be dissolved again. All worry about the self is vain; the ego is like a mirage, and all the tribulations that touch it

You cannot recognize lay Buddhists when you meet them in the street whether you are in Katmandu, Milton Keynes, Thailand or Tibet. Sometimes they wear white clothes when they go to temples and monasteries for special occasions, but usually their clothes are ordinary. Members of the monastic sangha, however, do wear special robes. These are saffron-coloured in Sri Lanka and Thailand, deep red in Tibet, and black in Japan. In this picture a western and a Japanese Zen Buddhist teacher mix happily and informally with a group of lay people whom they have been teaching at a Buddhist Society Summer School in Britain. There is an exchange of material and spiritual gifts: material gifts are given by the laity and the gift of the dharma by members of the sangha.

will pass away. They will vanish like a nightmare when the sleeper awakes ....
(Adapted from "The Going Forth" in *World of the Buddha*, edited by L. Stryk, Doubleday Anchor 1969.)

A SURPRISING LAYMAN

The Buddhist community has always included world-renouncers, who wear saffron robes, and householders or lay Buddhists, who often wear white for religious occasions. Vimalakirti was a remarkable layman about whom a whole Mahayana *sutra* is written. It is probably amongst some of the oldest Mahayana material we have.

Vimalakirti had the qualities of a *bodhisattva* (one who is on the path to full enlightenment) but chose to live as an ordinary layman in order to help others. When the text says he "converted" people, it means he helped them to lead a life more in keeping with truth and happiness, and pointed them in the direction of Nirvana. He had the skilful means (*upaya kausalya*) to do this.

He wore the white robes of a layman but observed the pure conduct of a recluse: he lived the household life but was not attached to the world. He had a wife and children but ever practised the religious life: he kept a household but ever delighted in solitude. . . .

He knew all businesses, but he took no pleasure in the worldly profits he gained. Rather he went out upon the streets to benefit all living creatures: he entered the courts to defend the oppressed; he attended the debates to lead the people to righteousness; he went to the schools to educate the untaught; he entered the brothels to show the follies of lust; he went to the wine houses to make firm the wills of men.
(From the *Vimalakirti – Nirdesa Sutra* quoted in *The Buddhist Experience*, by S. Beyer and G. Tucci, Dickenson 1974.)

A WAY OF INTELLIGENT REFLECTION

The style of teaching in Buddhism is reflective and not authoritarian. This extract is from a talk given by the Venerable Sumedho, Abbot of Amaravati Buddhist Centre.

> Buddhism offers a way of intelligent reflection on the human predicament. We all experience being born in the human form and having to ... experience all kinds of things, from the best to the worst, from pleasure to pain. . . . There is no one exempt from this experience of suffering, of growth, of ageing, of death. . . .
> There is not enough in the universe to truly satisfy, to give us complete satisfaction and complete contentment . . . . And this discontent, the Buddha pointed to very clearly, is due to the nature of the human mind itself. As long as we are ignorant – and I define this term as not knowing the truth about the way it is (in Buddhist terms not knowing the *dharma*) – then we operate from this self-view of me and mine, remain attached to this individual creature here . . . .

(From Amaravati Publication's *Personal Responsibility and the Nuclear Age* by the Venerable Sumedho 1987.)

HEARING THE DHARMA AND WAKING UP

When Gautama Buddha was asked who he was, he replied "I am awake". When he was living the best way of hearing the *dharma* and becoming fully awake, was by listening to his teaching. He did not always use words like those in the first section of this book. Zen Buddhists say that on one occasion he held up a flower and the one person who understood this action, smiled. Sometimes Gautama Buddha gave people a task to perform, and so helped them to see for themselves what they needed to know. In this way a person can learn from any activity or experience in life (if they are open to it) just as much as from sacred scriptures or sermons. But most people will hear the *dharma* in the conventional way by visiting a Dharma Centre, hearing a Buddhist teacher or reading about Buddhism.

Going to a Dharma Centre can make a considerable impression on children. There are monks and nuns in orange (saffron, the colour worn by Theravadins) or brown, and novices in white robes. White clothes are also worn by committed lay people. This little girl may be absorbed in a story she has just heard or be looking at a statue of the Buddha or watching some adults. Buddhists believe that if the seeds of the teaching are being sown in the right way, they will one day grow and bear fruit in this little girl's life.

GRIEVING AND UNDERSTANDING

Kisagotami is mentioned in the *Pali Canon* as one of Gautama Buddha's female followers. The commentaries on the canon tell an interesting story about the help he gave her when she was almost deranged with grief at the death of her child. He did not instruct her with words but gave her a task which he knew would help her to understand that suffering and death are built into our lives and that she was not alone in her experience. Kisagotami was desolate at the death of her son:

> In her grief she picked up the body of her child and wandered from one house to another, asking for medicine for her son.
> The people who met her laughed and sneered. "Whoever heard of medicine for the dead?" they said. . . .
> Kisagotami went to find the Buddha and stood on the edge of the crowd, listening to him. When she had the chance, she called out to him. "O, Exalted One, give me medicine for my son." Part of the Buddha's greatness was his skill in knowing how to help other people. He told her

kindly to go to the city nearby and visit every house. "Bring me some grains of mustard seed from every household in which no one has ever died."

Kisagotami was delighted. Here was someone who took her seriously. She went to the city, knocked on the first house and asked for some grains of mustard seed from the householder, if no one had ever died there. The householder told her with great sadness that he had recently lost his wife. Kisagotami listened to his story with growing sympathy, understanding his grief from her own. She eventually moved on, but found that in every house there was a story of sickness, old age and death. Her own grief seemed different now that she shared that of others, and she realized that the Buddha had known when he sent her out that she would find that her predicament was the common experience of human beings.

(From the *Pali Canon*, retold in *Buddhist Stories* by P. Morgan, Westminster College, Oxford.)

THE COLOURS OF MOSS

Nature produces an atmosphere that helps in the search for wisdom (*prajna*) and we should be prepared to read its messages even when it takes us away from our books. The following is a poem by Lin Tsung-yuan.

> I draw water from the well to wash my teeth
> and purify my mind as I brush my clothes.
> Idly turning the pages of my book
> I step out to the eastern library.
>
> I had hoped the words bequeathed to me would
> be profound,
> but how can one write down the true nature of
> things?
>
> But it is quiet here in the temple courtyard,
> where the colours of moss join the dense
> bamboos.
> The sun clears away the last of the morning mist
> and the green pines seem sleeked with oil.
>
> Weak and wordless I try to speak
> Realization floods my heart with rest.

(From *The Buddhist Experience*, by S. Beyer.)

COMING HOME

There are now a growing number of British Buddhists who follow one or other of the traditional schools, for example, the Theravada, Tibetan, Zen or Pure Land Schools. There is also a movement called the Western Buddhist Order and the Friends of the Western Buddhist Order, founded in 1967. Here, the founder of the order, Dennis Lingwood, who is now known as the Venerable Sangharakshita, describes how he first encountered the *dharma*.

> The paradoxical feeling of absolute newness and, at the same time, complete familiarity, is what many Western Buddhists experience, to a greater or lesser extent, on the occasion of their first contact with Buddhism, whether that contact takes the form of reading a Buddhist book, seeing an image of the Buddha, or paying a visit to a Buddhist spiritual community. They feel not just that they have gained something infinitely precious but that they have *regained* it. They feel that, after many wanderings, they have not only arrived at last at the gates of a glorious palace but also that, incredible as it seems, they have "come home". . . .

(Printed in *The Middle Way*, published by The Buddhist Society, November 1986.)

TAKING REFUGE

There are three precious things called jewels or refuges (*triratna*) in Buddhism. These three refuges are the *buddha*, the *dharma* and the *sangha*. A person becomes a member of the Buddhist community by "taking refuge" in these three. This involves repeating three phrases three times each. They are usually said in the traditional Buddhist languages such as Pali or Tibetan. In English the phrases are:

I go to the *buddha* for refuge (three times)
I go to the *dharma* for refuge (three times)
I go to the *sangha* for refuge (three times).

These words acknowledge the help and inspiration given by these three refuges in the Buddhist tradition. As it is the intention of the heart that matters for Buddhists, people can take refuge in their hearts without the knowledge of anyone else. It is also possible to say the formula privately, but it is thought best to say the words publically in a gathering of the whole community. Buddhists renew their commitment to these three precious things throughout their lives because the three refuges are taken at the beginning of most Buddhist meetings. They do not cancel out the need to make an effort on one's own. They help by providing an example to follow.

SAFETY AND DELIVERANCE

The *Dharmapada* is one of the most popular and famous collections of sayings in the *Pali Canon*. It is found in the *Sutra Pitaka* which contains the "threads" of Gautama Buddha's teachings. Here it explains that people try to find help and security in different ways, both by relying on many people, and in other ways during their lives, but that the best help is always to be found in the higher teachings of religious traditions.

> Men in their fear fly for refuge to mountains or forests, groves, sacred trees or shrines. But those are not a safe refuge, they are not the refuge that frees a man from sorrow.
>
> He who goes for refuge to Buddha, to Truth [*dharma*] and to those whom he taught [*sangha*], he goes indeed to a great refuge. Then he sees the four great truths:
>
> Sorrow, the cause of sorrow, the end of sorrow, and the path of eight stages which leads to the end of sorrow.
>
> That is the safe refuge, that is the refuge supreme. If a man goes to that refuge, he is free from sorrow.
>
> (From verses 188-192 of the *Dhammapada*, translated by J. Mascaro, Penguin 1973.)

Buddhists at Sigiriya in Sri Lanka put their hands together and sit low on the ground or kneel in a position of respect as they "take refuge". They are wearing the white clothes that lay Buddhists wear for religious ceremonies.

RESCUERS FROM SAMSARA

Most Buddhists practise the taking of the Three Refuges to help them progress from the cycles of birth, death and rebirth known as *samsara*, to Nirvana. Here is an extract from the work of a famous nineteenth-century Tibetan Buddhist teacher, Jamgon Kongtrul. He summarizes and comments on older teachings such as those of the eleventh-century Tibetan sGam-po-pa who devotes a whole chapter in his famous *Jewel Ornament of Liberation* to the subject of taking refuge.

> The following points should be understood in relation to Taking Refuge. In this world, we naturally seek someone capable of protecting us or providing refuge from causes of fear and anxiety, such as severe illness, and so on. Preoccupied by the countless fears which plague us throughout this life, and future lives, we could sink forever in the ocean of samsaric suffering. Neither our father, mother, relatives, friends, powerful gods nor similar beings are capable of giving us refuge from samsaric suffering. Nor are we ourselves capable of driving it off. If we do not find some effective source of refuge we will be utterly helpless. Only the Precious Ones have the ability to rescue us from *samsara*. Only those who can save themselves will be able to save others.

(Translated by J. Hanson, from *The Torch of Certainty*, by J. Kongtrul, Shambhala Publications 1977.)

A CONSTANT ACT OF LEARNING

Here a modern Theravada Buddhist talks about the way we learn constantly from referring our attitudes and lives to the standards set by the *buddha*, the *dharma* and the *sangha*. These all show us the qualities of morality (*sila*), meditation (*samadhi*) and wisdom (*prajna*).

> Refuge can be taken at various levels. If refuge is taken in the sense of discipleship, life becomes a constant act of learning, of adapting the mind to the standards set by the *buddha*, the *dharma* and the *sangha*. It is the character of the wise man that he is always willing and anxious to learn. The process of learning establishes a mutual relationship between teacher, teaching and pupil, such that a gradual and partial identification takes place and the pupil can absorb the teacher's wisdom and make it his own.

(From *The Vision of Dharma* by Nyanaponika Thera, Century Hutchinson 1986.)

MAKING OFFERINGS TO THE BUDDHA

Buddhists honour Siddhartha Gautama because he made a great effort to discover the ancient noble path to enlightenment and then to show it to others. When they see an image of him or any of the Buddhas (enlightened beings) in a shrine room they are inspired by it. He was human like us, but the serenely smiling face and calm body of his images show super human loving kindness, compassion, sympathetic joy and equanimity.

These qualities are called the four *brahma viharas* and are four sublime states of mind which all Buddhists hope to attain. Bringing and offering flowers in a shrine room adds to the sense of beauty and happiness created there as do incense and light. Flowers also show love and respect for the memory of the Buddha. From their symbolic fragility a lesson can be learnt which in itself reinforces the Buddha's message.

SCATTERING BLOSSOMS

You will often see pictures of Gautama Buddha reclining on his right side (see "Accepting Death"). This is how he lay down between two sala trees when he was dying. Some of the stories say that when he was born and when he died, nature honoured him with flowers and perfumed water. This account is from the *sutra* about his death in the *Pali Canon*.

Now on that occasion the twin sala trees were quite covered with blossoms though it was not in season. They scattered and sprinkled and strewed them on the Blessed One's body out of veneration for him. And heavenly flowers and heavenly sandalwood powder fell from the sky and were scattered and sprinkled and strewed over the Blessed One's body out of veneration for him. And heavenly music was played and heavenly songs were sung in the sky out of veneration for him.

(From *The Life of the Buddha*, by Bhikkhu Nanamoli, Buddhist Publication Society 1978.)

SPOILING A GOLDEN BUDDHA

Having the right intentions when you do anything is crucial for Buddhists. Good acts with mean or selfish motives spoil the effect. Wanting to keep the incense for your own Buddha and quite apart from the Buddhas honoured by other people is a form of greed and ignorance. The Buddha nature should be honoured wherever it is found. Your own attitudes have a way of being reflected back at you.

A nun who was searching for enlightenment made a statue of Buddha and covered it with

This young woman is bringing flowers as an offering to the Buddha. She shows her respect for the memory of the Buddha in the way she kneels and holds her hands, as well as in the words she says.

gold leaf. Wherever she went she carried the golden Buddha with her.

Years passed and, still carrying her Buddha, the nun came to live in a small temple in a country where there were many Buddhas, each one with its own particular shrine.

The nun wished to burn incense before her golden Buddha. Not liking the idea of the perfume straying to the others, she devised a funnel through which the smoke would ascend only to her statue. This blackened the nose of the golden Buddha making it especially ugly.

(From *Zen Flesh, Zen Bones*, P. Reps, Penguin 1971.)

REMEMBERING NOT PRAYING: IT'S THE THOUGHT THAT COUNTS

The Buddha was a human being, although an extraordinary one. He is now dead and has passed into the state of Nirvana beyond our reach. This means he cannot answer our prayers. Remembering the story of his life and his achievements can, however, encourage and help others towards Nirvana. There is no better way of remembering him than looking at his statue.

Prayer doesn't exist in Buddhism because there's no one to talk to. In my devotions I say to myself "To the best of my ability, I shall try to emulate the life of the Buddha." So I have my shrine-room, and even my children before they go to work or their colleges, they do their devotion, and only after their devotion, they set out.

It's almost the same as having a portrait of your parents to remind you of the love that they had for you.

(From the words of Dr Fernando in J. Bowker, *Worlds of Faith*, BBC Enterprises, 1983.)

FOLLOWING THE PATH

Making a journey, setting off on a spiritual pilgrimage, is an important part of being a Buddhist. The fourth Noble Truth explains that there is a path from suffering to Nirvana, the end of suffering. It consists of right understanding, right thought, right speech, right action, right livelihood, right effort, right mindfulness, and right concentration.

A journey along a path is a means of getting from one place to another, not just an end in itself. The broad description of what makes a good "path" does not mean that all ways have to be the same. Some people can find their own way up a mountain; while others follow the gentle track worn by centuries of experienced travellers, and there are those who dare to scale rock faces, roped to a good guide.

Another image that Buddhists use in describing the journey to Nirvana, is that of crossing a river. To cross *samsara*, the river of birth and death, we need a boat or a raft and possibly a ferryman. While the word *vada* (as in Theravada) is usually translated as way, *yana* (as in Mahayana) is translated as vehicle or boat. When the Buddha used the image of a raft, he emphasized that it was made for a specific purpose, and that having served its purpose, it should not be carried about, but put on one side. Teachings (the paths) are not to be clung to for their own sake, but for the way they can help the pupil to the "further shore", which is Nirvana.

It may not be easy to find and follow a path if you do not have a guide or a map of some kind. Older Buddhists, both lamas *(religious teachers) and parents have the responsibility of showing young Buddhists the paths that are available in their religion. This involves learning to read and understand Buddhist texts but also learning how to live a moral life, how to meditate, recite* mantras *and pray together.*

FOLLOWING THE PATH

FORESTS, SWAMPS AND PRECIPICES

Finding a teacher who is skilful in showing them a path is one of the most important things for a Buddhist. Gautama Buddha is an obvious example of such a teacher. The teacher needs to be wiser than the pupil, which means both that he or she is further along the path to enlightenment than the pupil, and also that he or she is able to understand the best way for the pupil to travel along the path. There has been a succession of teachers throughout Buddhist history and all the schools of Buddhism have living teachers preserving and transmitting the *dharma* today. This is the main duty of the monastic *sangha*, although teachers do not have to be monks or nuns. In this story from the *Pali Canon* Gautama Buddha explains some of these ideas to Tissa, one of his pupils.

> "Suppose now, Tissa, there be two men, one unskilled in the way, the other skilled in the way. And the one who is unskilled asks the way of the other who is skilled in the way. And that other replies: 'Yes, this is the way, sir. When you have gone by it for a short time you will see that it divides into two paths. Leave the left one and take the one to the right. Go on for a little and you will see a thick forest. Go on for a little and you will see a great marshy swamp. Go on for a little and you will see a steep precipice. Go on for a little and you will see a delightful stretch of level ground.'
>
> "Such is my parable, Tissa, to show my meaning; and this is what it means: By the 'man who is unskilled in the way' is meant the many-folk [ordinary people]. By the 'man who is skilled in the way' is meant . . . [a Buddha]. By 'dividing into two paths' is meant a state of wavering. 'The way to the left' means the wrong eightfold way . . . . The 'thick forest', Tissa, is a name for ignorance. The 'great marshy swamp' is a name for pleasures of the senses. The 'steep precipice' is . . . anger. The 'delightful stretch of level ground' is a name for Nirvana."
>
> (Quoted in World of the Buddha, edited by L. Stryk.)

A SKILFUL GUIDE

The *Lotus Sutra* is one of the most famous scriptures of Mahayana Buddhism. It contains many stories about the help that is given to all sorts of people trying to find a path to enlightenment. The help they are given is not always obvious and straightforward. In one story a father rescues his sons who are unknowingly trapped in a burning house by using a "trick" or device to get them to come out of it. He promises them a present which he knows they want. When they rush out to find the promised present he gives them something even better than his promise. Another story describes how a different father disguises himself as a servant so that he can talk to his destitute son as a fellow worker.

In the following story a guide uses skilful means (*upaya kausalya*) to keep a group of travellers on their journey when they are lost and too tired to continue their search for "precious jewels".

> There is a steep, difficult, very bad road, five hundred *yojanas* in length, empty and devoid of human beings — a frightful place. There is a great multitude wishing to traverse this road to arrive at a cache of precious jewels. There is a guide, perceptive and wise, of penetrating clarity, who knows the hard road, its passable and impassable features, and who, wishing to get through these hardships, leads the multitude. The multitude being led get disgusted midway and say to the guide, "We are exhausted, and also

frightened; we cannot go on. It is still a long way off, and we now wish to turn back." The guide, being a man of many skilful devices, thinks: "These wretches are to be pitied! How can they throw away a fortune in jewels and wish instead to turn back?" When he has had this thought, with his power of devising expedients he conjures up on that steep road, three hundred *yojanas* away, a city, then he declares to the multitude, "Have no fear! There is no need to turn back! Here is this great city. You may stop in it and do as you please. . . ."

At that time, the exhausted multitude, overjoyed at heart, sigh as at something they have never had before, saying, "We have escaped that bad road, and shall quickly regain our composure." Thereupon the multitude proceed to enter the conjured city. . . . At that time, the guide, knowing that the multitude have rested and are no longer fatigued, straightway dissolves the conjured city and says to the multitude, "Come away! The jewel cache is near. The great city of a while ago was conjured up by me for the purpose of giving you a rest, nothing more."

(Translated by L. Hurvitz in *Scripture of the Lotus Blossom of the Fine Dharma*, Columbia University Press 1976.)

THE WAY THROUGH AMIDA'S LAND

A special school of Buddhism, developed in China in the fifth century CE, teaches that you can be reborn in the Buddha Amitabha's realm if you repeat his name with faith, thus showing your confidence in his enlightened compassion. Once you are reborn in the Pure Land, Amitabha is such a skilful teacher and conditions are so sympathetic that you are sure to reach Nirvana soon. Pure Land Buddhism reached Japan in the sixth and seventh centuries CE and still flourishes there. The Japanese phrase used for the *nembutsu* (name of Buddha) is *Namu Amida Butsu*: Homage to Amida Buddha. Here a Japanese businessman in Hawaii talks about the way he follows the path of the Pure Land school in his daily life.

"As a business man, I do not know the why and whereofs of the technicalities of the Buddhist religion, but I know that with complete and full trust in the teachings and the universal truth of Buddhism, I can find peace and solace from the business world.

"My mornings start with the changing of the water for the flowers at the altar, lighting the candles, offering hot tea and incense, and reciting "Namu Amida Butsu" with a "Good morning, I will be going to work." I thank and appreciate the fact that I am well and ready for another day. At night, hot rice is offered in the container of brass, and "Namu Amida Butsu" is repeated with "I am home." Before I go to bed, I once again repeat the nembutsu (Namu Amida Butsu). These are simple rituals but the importance of going through these rituals is the peace and the feeling of complete trust I have in my heart and the sense of appreciation of well being.

"In religion, I have found the beauty of appreciation, understanding, and the staunch and unchanging faith to entrust myself to Lord Buddha."

(From *Hawaii Buddhism* No. 729, July 1985 published by the Hawaii Council of Jodo Missions.)

TAKING THE PRECEPTS

Morality (*sila*) is one of the basic stages of the Noble Eightfold Path. Right speech, right action and right livelihood are particularly important. What is "right" is what is appropriate in any particular situation. There is also a basic list of ten precepts which expand these areas in more detail.

1. I undertake the rule of training to refrain from harming any living things.
2. I undertake the rule of training to refrain from taking what is not given.
3. I undertake the rule of training to refrain from a misuse of the senses, i.e. unchastity.
4. I undertake the rule of training to refrain from wrong speech.
5. I undertake the rule of training to refrain from taking drugs or drinks which tend to cloud the mind.
6. I undertake the rule of training to refrain from taking food at an unseasonable time, i.e. after the midday meal (lunch).
7. I undertake the rule of training to refrain from dancing, music, singing and unseemly shows.
8. I undertake the rule of training to refrain from the use of garlands, perfumes, unguents, and from things that tend to beautify and adorn (the person).
9. I undertake the rule of training to refrain from using high and luxurious seats (and beds).
10. I undertake the rule of training to refrain from accepting gold and silver.

The precepts are not understood as commands but as ways of behaving which are helpful for making spiritual progress. Both body, speech and mind should ideally be involved in one's *sila*. Lay Buddhists voluntarily take the first five precepts as a basis for everyday life. There is a chance to re-take them at most Buddhist meetings. It is also possible for lay Buddhists to undertake eight or all ten precepts for special reasons or on special days, for example when they are on a meditation retreat or visiting a Dharma Centre for a festival. Novice monks and nuns undertake eight precepts. Theravada nuns live on all ten precepts; monks take not only ten precepts but observe at least 227 other rules of life from the *Vinaya Pitaka*.

BETTER THAN A GIFT

Living by the precepts is seen as a way to become happy and to help others to be happy too. The individual is free to take or give back the vows as he or she feels able to live by them. Monks and nuns who undertake more precepts than the laity often seem to be some of the happiest people around. A sacrifice is really a gift freely given – a present. The negative aspect is that someone has to part with it, but the positive side is being on the receiving end. This is how the Buddha is said to have talked about morality, explaining it as being better than a gift.

"How can a man's conduct be good? .... By putting away all unkindness to living things he abstains from destroying life. He lays aside the

TAKING THE PRECEPTS

... sword and, full of humility and pity, he is compassionate and kind to all creatures that have life. Putting away the desire for things which are not his, he does not take anything that is not freely given him .... He passes his life in honesty and in purity of heart .... Putting away all thought of deceiving .... he speaks truthfully .... he never injures his fellow men by deceit ....

"He brings together those who are divided, he encourages those who are friendly; he is a peacemaker, a lover of peace, impassioned for peace, a speaker of words that make for peace ...."

(The *Tevigga Sutra*, from *World of the Buddha*, edited by L. Stryk.)

MANY KINDS OF KILLING

This is a Zen Buddhist story from one of the many anecdotal collections made of the sayings of the Japanese Zen Buddhist masters. It shows that killing is as much an aggressive and destructive attitude of mind and heart as an external action. Gasan is the name of the master.

Gasan instructed his adherents one day: "Those who speak against killing and who desire to spare the lives of all conscious beings are right. It is good to protect even animals and insects. But what about those persons who kill time, what about those who are destroying wealth, and those who destroy political economy? We should not overlook them. Furthermore, what of the one who preaches without enlightenment? He is killing Buddhism."

(From *Zen Flesh, Zen Bones*, by P. Reps.)

TRIPLE VALUES

Santoka Taneda (1882-1940), who wrote the following poem, was a Zen master who wrote a journal about the years at the end of his life when he had renounced the world and travelled about living as close to nature as he could. He wrote a lot of *haiku*, which is a Japanese form of poetry.

My Three Precepts:
Do not waste anything.
Do not get angry.
Do not complain.

My Three Vows:
Do not attempt the impossible.
Do not feel regret for the past.
Do not berate oneself.

My Three Joys:
Study.
Contemplation.
Haiku.

The first precept is about not harming living things. This involves positive actions as well as restraint. Buddhists try to make sure that every living creature has its chance to live. Particularly at festivals, Buddhists in countries such as Thailand buy caged birds and fish in bowls. Then, like the woman in this picture, they make an offering of their action at a temple and let the bird out of its cage or release the fish into a river. This is an action of great merit as well as a way of keeping the precepts.

CHOOSING THE RIGHT LIVELIHOOD

Right livelihood is one of the areas of morality recommended by the Noble Eightfold Path. What is right is what is appropriate in particular situations and this is decided in conjunction with other aspects of Buddhist ethics such as the Five Precepts.

The occupations traditionally discouraged, involve anything dealing in:

1. arms
2. living beings, for example slaves
3. flesh, for example being a butcher
4. intoxicating drinks
5. poisons

THERE IS NEVER A TIME WHEN NO ONE SEES

This story is taken from the collection of *Jataka* tales in the *Pali Canon*. It describes how the Buddha reacted in a previous birth when he was asked to rely on stealing for a livelihood.

> One day a master told his pupils that he was growing old and frail and that they must provide what he needed to live. The pupils were worried because the people in the town were mean and they knew it was pointless to ask them for help. The master told them that as his was a deserving cause it would not be wrong for them to take the money that they needed rather than ask for it. The pupils said that they would do anything for their master, and so he encouraged them to plan to take rich men's purses and steal from travellers. However he made them promise two things: firstly that they would not hurt anyone and secondly that they would make sure they were never seen.
>
> They were all eager to start, except for one pupil. He stood in silence with his head downcast. The teacher asked him why he was not eager to begin. Like the others, did he not love his teacher? The pupil begged his master for forgiveness but said that what he asked was impossible. "Why?" asked the old man. "Because there is never a time when no one sees. I see what I am doing, and I should be ashamed. I will take a bowl and beg for you but I will not steal." When he said this the teacher's face lit up. He embraced the boy and said how happy he was to have such a pupil. He told the others that this boy had really been listening to his teaching. The others hung their heads in shame.

(From the *Jataka* tales of the *Pali Canon*, retold in *Buddhist Stories*, by P. Morgan.)

This young woman is working on very modern letter-setting equipment for Windhorse Publications, one of the Friends of the Western Buddhist Order's "right livelihood" co-operatives. At first sight her room looks like any other office, but in the foreground she has a small shrine with some flowers which reminds her that her work is done within the framework of her Buddhist commitment.

21
CHOOSING THE RIGHT LIVELIHOOD

LIVING IN HARMONY

P'ang Yun was a Chinese layman who lived between about 740 and 808 CE. He belonged to the Chinese Ch'an (Zen in Japanese) Buddhist tradition. Accounts of his life show how he lived very contentedly with his wife and their children in times of revolution and great change. The anecdotes about him were put together after his death by his friend Yu Ti. The ordinariness of his life is summarized in the famous final phrase of the following extract "drawing water and carrying firewood". This is his "marvellous" livelihood which contrasts with the high offices of the government officials who wear vermilion and purple.

One day Shih-T'ou said to the Layman (P'ang): "Since seeing me, what have your daily activities been?"

"My daily activities are not unusual
I'm just naturally in harmony with them.
Grasping nothing, discarding nothing,
In every place there's no hindrance, no conflict.
Who assigns the ranks of vermilion and purple?
The hills and mountains' last speck of dust is extinguished.
My supernatural power and marvellous activity —
Drawing water and carrying firewood."
(From *The Recorded Sayings of Layman P'ang*, John Weatherhill 1971.)

CO-OPERATING WITH OTHERS

The Friends of the Western Buddhist Order have tried to put right livelihood into practice with co-operative work ventures. These include a building team, a printing press, a wholefood shop and restaurant and an import wholesalers. The co-operatives support their members financially and in wider human ways. They help support the *dharma* teaching and meditation centres of the Western Buddhist Order and their friends in general.

> No work shall be engaged in which causes harm to other beings. Apart from obviously harmful pursuits such as the manufacture of armaments, we interpret this as including anything which exploits other beings, whether by deceit, force, or by playing upon negative emotions, or which damages, destroys, or pollutes the environment or wastes the earth's natural resources. On the contrary, goods and services shall be provided which enhance life and help people to develop. No worker shall gain more than enough to cover his work. The principle to be followed is to give what one can and to take what one needs. . . .
> No-one shall be subject to another and the needs of all shall be equally considered. However, it is to be recognised that some people have greater experience and ability both practically and as human beings and it is to these people that we shall look for guidance. . . .
> Above all, we shall endeavour to bear in mind at all times that the fundamental consideration behind everything we do is the development of individuals. We shall always examine what we do in this light and ensure that, through the functioning of the Co-operative, we ourselves are developing and contributing to the growth of all beings.

(From *Buddhism For Today*, by D. Subhuti, Windhouse Publications, 1988.)

BEING IN A FAMILY

Ideally we all begin life in a family that teaches us basic morality and loving kindness. The *Dharmapada* says:

**To have a mother is happiness in the world
To have a father is happiness in the world**

But although the love within a family is an important example that Buddhists quote, and it is not impossible to become enlightened while being married and having children, Buddhists think that it is more difficult to follow a spiritual path as a lay person than as a world-renouncer. Lay morality is focused more on gaining a better rebirth than on enlightenment. But Buddhists still say that every situation (even marriage) is a path to enlightenment, as long as one is mindful. The modern Tibetan teacher, Chogyam Trungpa, points out that before the world's problems can be solved, people must put their own households in order first. A marriage represents the principle of sharing and making love can be as much an expression of gentleness, understanding and appreciation as of sensuality, greed and power.

A Buddhist family inside their home in Eastern Bhutan. The family are paper makers and everyone that is old enough helps with the work. Their relationships are relaxed, affectionate, loyal and happy.

SERVING THOSE WE LOVE

The *Sigalavada Sutra* in the *Pali Canon* gives very full advice about relationships within the family.

> ... a child should minister to his parents.... [saying] "Once supported by them I will now be their support; I will perform duties incumbent on them; I will keep up the lineage and tradition of my family; I will make myself worthy of my heritage."
> In five ways parents thus ministered to ... by their child, show their love for him: they restrain him from vice, they exhort him to virtue, they train him to a profession, they contract a suitable marriage for him, and in due time they hand over his inheritance.
> ... In five ways should a wife ... be ministered to by her husband: by respect, by courtesy, by faithfulness, by handing over authority to her, by providing her with adornment.
> In these five ways does the wife, ministered to by her husband ... love him: her duties are well performed, by hospitality to the kin of both, by faithfulness, by watching over the goods he brings, and by skill and industry in discharging all her business.

(The *Sigalavada Sutra*, from *The Buddha's Philosophy of Man*, by T. Ling, Dent 1981.)

REMEMBERING MOTHERS

The Tibetan teacher sGam-po-pa summarizes centuries of teaching about the inspiring role of mothers and how our love for all other beings should be based on the model of the relationship between a mother and her children. sGam-po-pa lived between 1079 and 1153 CE. His *Jewel Ornament of Liberation* deals with the whole of Buddhism as a way of life. This extract is from chapter 11, which discusses benevolence and compassion.

> In this life here on earth the greatest benefactor is our mother, because she (i) provides us with a body, (ii) suffers for our sake, (iii) gives us life and (iv) shows us the world....
> The benefit of going through hardships for our sake means that [our mother] ... not only dressed and adorned us, but gave us her inheritance, keeping nothing of her own, not even a crumb, giving us all her food and drink, so that when we set out for foreign parts we should not suffer from hunger and thirst, giving us clothes to keep out the cold and money to prevent our pining in poverty. Unlike people who, because they do not want a thing, give it to a child, she allows herself a minimum of food, drink and clothing. A mother does not do things for the sake of happiness in this life, nor refrains from action for the sake of enjoyment in the hereafter, she just nurses and protects her baby....
>
> If one individual were to transform all the earth, stones, trees and groves in this world into single juniper kernels, another might well be able to finish counting them. But no one can count what his mother has done for him.

(The *Jewel Ornament of Liberation*, by sGam-po-pa, translated by H.V. Guenther, Rider & Co. 1959.)

JOURNEYING TOGETHER

Marriage is a civil and legal contract for Buddhists and traditionally there is no service or ceremony at a *vihara* involving monks and nuns. It might seem inappropriate or even inauspicious for them to be involved in such a worldly occasion. However, in countries such as Sri Lanka as well as in the west, Buddhists now like to have a "religious" ceremony. Most Buddhists make up their own form of service which includes the legal contract. Here is a prayer from a service printed by the Buddhist Society some years ago. The "Triple Jewel" is the *Buddha*, the *dharma* and the *sangha*.

Remembering that all things are impermanent and Life itself is therefore filled with suffering, know you and forget not that when passion dies and earthly interests have passed away, this Triple Jewel shall remain to link your lives in one; the All-Enlightened One who pointed out the Way, the Message of Enlightenment he gave, and the Glorious Company of those who follow in the Way. Such and such alone is the triple strand which binds you and will ever bind, until, self-perfected and free, you enter hand-in-hand the silence of Nirvana.

Therefore, let your love for one another be as the love between two Pilgrims on the self-same Way, sharing alike your joys and sorrows and the thousand incidents that form the karmic burden of a bygone day, in all things sympathetic, helpful, courteous to one another, caring only for each other's welfare and the common weal.

(From *Buddhism in England* Vol.II No 6, published by the Buddhist Society.)

MEDITATING

Meditation doesn't just involve sitting on the floor in the Lotus position and becoming oblivious to the world. The most important aspect of meditation for Buddhists is being mindful and attentive, and this can be done in any position. Meditating is a form of interior pilgrimage to find the truth about the way things are. Facing reality – and it involves just that – can be a traumatic challenge, but with the help of a skilful teacher, qualities of loving kindness, compassion, sympathetic joy and equanimity (the four *brahma-viharas*) will begin to establish themselves.

A Japanese Zen monk meditates in a garden at Kyoto. A Zen garden, made of rocks and raked sand, is a miniature representation of the outside world, with mountains, sea and land. The sea in particular is used as an image for Nirvana, and meditating in such a garden enables a Buddhist to see reality in perspective.

COMPOSED AND ATTENTIVE

Lay people practise meditation as much as they can but may not be as skilled as monks and nuns. In Theravada Buddhism particularly, meditation is often referred to as the "work" of the monk who devotes a great deal of time to it. The following passage from the *Pali Canon* reflects these ideas.

>Whether he walk or stand or rest or lie
>Or stretch his limbs or draw them in again,
>Let him do all these things composedly;
>Above, across, and back again returning —
>Whatever be one's bourn in all the world —
>Let him be one who views the rise-and-fall
>Of all compounded things attentively.
>So dwelling ardent, living a life of peace
>And not elated, but to calmness given,
>For mind's composure doing what is right,
>Ever and always training,—"ever intent" —
>That is the name men give to such a monk.

(From *The World of Buddhism*, edited by L. Stryk.)

SEEING REALITY FACE TO FACE

Here is an extract from a classical text by the Mahayana teacher Kamalasila who lived in the eighth century CE. It is called *Bhavanakrama*, or *The Stages of Meditation*. It is still a standard guidebook for Mahayana Buddhists. It reveals that meditation is built on a life of virtue (*sila*) and that it is motivated by compassion for the sufferings of the world.

>And thus he who wishes to see reality face-to-face should set out to meditate.
>
>*Calm.* First he should practise calm, that he may steady his mind: for the mind is as wavering as water, and is not steady without the support of calm; and he cannot know things as they really are with a mind unconcentrated. As the Blessed One has said: "It is a concentrated mind which understands things as they really are."
>
>Should his mind become depressed, and overcome by drowsiness and torpor, which keep him from clearly grasping the meditative object, he should calm his depression with a less abstract meditation, concentrating perhaps on such a pleasing theme as the virtues of the Buddhas and bodhisattvas; and he should then grasp the meditative object all the more firmly.
>
>Should he find that his mind is becoming a bit giddy through remembering past laughter and delight, he should calm its giddiness by concentrating upon something sobering, such as impermanence; and he should then exert himself upon the meditative object, with his mind flowing evenly and naturally.
>
>And when he finds that his mind is detached from depression and giddiness, and is flowing smoothly and spontaneously, he should relax all effort; for to make any effort when his mind is flowing smoothly would only distract it.
>
>And when his mind is thus flowing evenly and naturally upon the meditative object, he can continue as long as he wishes: and he should know that his calm is then made perfect. . . .
>
>This is the way of calm which the Blessed One has taught us in scripture.

(From *The Buddhist Experience*, edited by S. Beyer and G. Tucci.)

FINDING JOY

The careful discipline and exactness which is needed in the early stages of meditation eventually give way to a natural, easy spontaneity. This is both a result of and one of the characteristics of a meditator's life. It is expressed in the songs of the Tibetan Milarepa (1040-1123 CE). He rejoices in nature. His solitariness is not miserable and oppressive but an occasion for bubbling happiness.

   this mountain land is a joyful place
   a land of meadows & bright flowers

   the trees dance in the forest
   a place where monkeys play

   where birds sing all manner of song
   and bees whirl & hover

   day and night a rainbow flashes
   summer and winter a sweet rain falls
   spring and autumn a mist rolls in

   and in such solitude as this
   the cotton clad Mila finds his joy

            " " "

   and I have lost my taste for crowds
   to gain my freedom in solitude

have given up bother
to be happy in loneliness

have given up family
to possess nothing at all

I do not seek wisdom in books
content to leave my mind alone

nor seek to better myself through talking
content to leave my mouth alone

nor know how to cheat and lie
content to leave the world alone

nor proudly scratch for fame
content when no one speaks of me

any place I stay is all right
whatever happens I am happy

any clothes I wear are all right
whatever you do I am happy

any food I eat is all right
whatever occurs I am happy

("The Biography of Cotton-Clad Mila", ed. Sangs-rgyas-gyal-mtshan, in *The Buddhist Experience*, edited by S. Beyer.)

JOINING THE SANGHA

The word *sangha* is most commonly used for the monastic part of the Buddhist community, although originally it meant all Buddhists, both lay and monastic. Buddhists never say that it is impossible to be enlightened as a lay person leading an ordinary life. The ideal of constant mindfulness and attentiveness is possible in any situation and so is the freeing of the heart from attachment, as in the case of Vimalakirti (see page 7). Most Buddhists, however, think that the life of a monk or nun is a higher path and is the most likely to lead to a good rebirth and enlightenment. *Sangha* discipline is strict and in terms of material possessions life might seem hard, but one famous verse from the *Dharmapada* says very positively: "Let us be happy then, we who possess nothing."

This is the sima, or ordination area in the garden of Chithurst Forest monastery in Sussex. It is made in the traditional way. A group of senior Theravada monks are about to accept the request of two novices to become full members of the monastic sangha. They will then change from their white robes into the saffron ones they are carrying on their arms.

AT EASE AND CONTENTED

All ways of life bring their different rewards. King Ajatasattu was interested in the way of life of the world-renouncers at the time of the Buddha. He took some courtiers and went into the forest to find Gautama Buddha and his followers and question them about their life.

"And how . . . is the [bhikshu] content? The [bhikshu] is satisfied with sufficient robes to cover his body, with sufficient food to keep him alive. Wherever he may go these he takes with him as he goes — just as a bird with his wings, wherever he may fly. So the [bhikshu] lives content.

"Then, having . . . gained this excellent self-restraint as to the senses, endowed with this excellent mindfulness and self-possession, filled with this excellent content, he chooses some lonely spot where he can rest on his way — in the woods, at the foot of a tree, on a hill side, in a mountain glen, in a rocky cave . . . . Returning there after his round for alms he seats himself, when his meal is done, cross-legged, keeping his body erect, and his intelligence alert, intent.

"Putting away all hankering after the world . . . putting away the corrupting wish to injure, he remains with a mind free from ill-temper . . . . Putting away flurry and worry, he remains free from fretfulness . . . . Putting away wavering, he remains . . . no longer in suspense as to what is good, he purifies his mind of doubt.

. . .

"And gladness springs up within him on his realizing that, and joy arises to him, gladdened as he is, and so rejoicing all his body becomes at ease, and being at ease he is filled with a sense of peace, and in that peace his heart is stayed."
(The *Sammana-phala Sutra* from *The Buddha's Philosophy of Man* by T. Ling.)

MUTUAL HELP AND SERVICE

Life in a monastery is very traditional and often goes on in the same way for centuries. D.T. Suzuki was a Japanese scholar who lived from 1870-1966. He did a great deal to inspire interest and knowledge about Buddhism, especially Zen Buddhism, in the West. He did this through books, lectures, travelling and making friends. One of the books he wrote is called *The Training of A Zen Buddhist Monk* which is based on the routine at the Engaku-ji in Kamakura. Although Dr Suzuki was a layman he had experience of monastic training and the way that life in a monastery integrates the rhythms of work, study, eating and meditation into a whole. This extract shows the calm structure of life but also the sense of a caring community. It begins by describing what is done at the main meal time.

. . . the prayer is offered that the meal be equally shared by all sentient beings . . . .

The five subjects of meditation are then repeated:
(1) Do we really merit this offering? (2) We are seriously made to think about our own virtues; (3) The object is to detach ourselves from the fault of greed and other defects; (4) Meal is to be taken as medicine in order to keep the body healthy and strong; (5) We accept this meal so as to make ourselves fit receptacles for the truth. The Five Meditations are followed by these vows: The first morsel is for destroying all evils; the second morsel is for practising all deeds of goodness; the third morsel is for delivering all beings so that we all finally attain Buddhahood.

No words are uttered during the course of eating, everything goes on silently and in the most orderly sequence. The waiters are monks themselves taking their turn. When finished, the head-monk claps the wooden blocks. The bowls are quietly washed at the table and wiped and put up in a piece of cloth which is carried by each monk. While this is going on, some verses are recited. When the hand-bell is struck, the diners all stand and walk back to their Hall in perfect order.

When a monk is sick and cannot stand the Zendo life, he is taken into a separate room called *Enjudo* ("life-prolonging room") where he is nursed by a fellow-monk. It is thus that the young novitiate begins to learn how to serve his fellow-monks. In graver cases the patient will of course be sent to a hospital where he is with due care looked after.

(Quoted in *Buddhism* by R. Gard, Prentice Hall 1961.)

PUTTING ONE FOOT IN FRONT OF THE OTHER

Most monks and nuns live in settled communities like the monastery described in the last section. But one expression of monastic renunciation is called *dhutanga* (*tudong* in Thai). This is a means of shaking off attachment to the world and can refer to the custom of walking for weeks, months or even years, carrying just the basic monastic possessions: an almsbowl, a spare set of robes, a razor, sewing equipment, a water jar and an umbrella with a mosquito net, or in this country a small tent. Verse nine of the *Dharmapada* talks about mindfulness as not being attached to a home:

Like swans that abandon the lake
They leave home after home behind.

Here is a description by an English Theravada *bhikshu*, the Venerable Sucitto, of the end of a period of walking *dhutanga*.

He and his companion are returning to Chithurst Forest Monastery in Sussex.

When the walk came to an end, thirteen mornings after leaving, the practice-path that it symbolises continued: the monastic life is about non-abiding, it is a giving up of personal possessions, desires, concerns and opinions. You listen and live close to the heart of life, and the only refuge from the rawness of our nature is to do good and be mindful. Sometimes that seems to leave you completely alone with nothing to hold on to, but the path evokes a compassion in us that fills the heart, and a respect for our way of life that gives us many friends. Before we reached the monastery, we stopped to say hello to Sam, the woodsman who works in the barn at the top of Chithurst Lane. "You've just got back, have you?" he said, "Please, just wait a moment." He walked to the back of his workshop and returned with half of his packed lunch. "Can I put this into your bowl?"

(From *Cittaviveka* published by The Chithurst Forest Monastery, 1983.)

CELEBRATING FESTIVALS

Festivals bring laypeople and the monastic *sangha* together on a larger scale than during the course of everyday life. Both sides are generous in what they have to give. The laity offer food and robes to the monks and nuns. The *sangha* gives spiritual friendship and the gift of the *dharma*.

Buddhist festivals are not required by or described in the sacred texts themselves, although many of the events and activities they celebrate are linked with events in the Buddha's life, particularly his birth, enlightenment and death, and activities he recommended.

For most Buddhists the calendar of festivals is a lunar one and the most important occasions all take place at the time of a full moon. These festivals are different in each of the main Buddhist traditions or even in each Buddhist country. In the Theravada countries of Sri Lanka, Burma and Thailand there is a very important festival which is called after the Sri Lankan month *Wesak*, also called *Vesakha-puja*, or Buddha Day. This is usually in May in Britain. Buddha Day celebrates the birth, enlightenment and death of Gautama Buddha all at the same time. The Tibetan Mahayana traditions have a similar occasion at a different time.

In Mahayana Japan the dates are now on a fixed calendar and the birth of the Buddha is celebrated at *Hana Matsuri* on 8 April. The enlightenment is remembered on 8 December at *Jodo-e* and the death at *Nehan-e* on 15 February.

Most countries also have their own New Year festivals like the colourful Tibetan *Losar*. Another important celebration is that which ends the rainy season retreat, the *Vassa*. This festival is named after the robe on which the ceremony focuses, the *kathina*. Lay Buddhists bring cloth for robes and any other large items that might be needed by the monks during the next year. (See "Giving Generously".)

During all festivals there is a sense of being on holiday and in Britain people get together during the nearest weekend to the full moon day. They usually congregate at the Dharma Centres and there is a lot of *dana*, generous giving, usually in the form of sharing food with the monastic community and all other guests.

THE FULL MOON OF ENLIGHTENMENT

None of the most sacred Buddhist scriptures contain a full biography of Gautama Buddha. The first continuous account of his life is in Sanskrit and was written in the first century CE by the Indian poet Ashvaghosha. It is called the 'Acts of the Buddha' or *Buddhacarita*. It describes the Buddha's enlightenment, and captures the atmosphere of a festival very well. Mara, the evil one, who is linked with death and despair, is defeated. His arrows are turned into lotus blossoms and the whole world seems to rejoice. This is the spirit of both *Wesak* and *Jodo-e*.

> The great seer, free from the dust of passion, victorious over darkness' gloom, had vanquished Mara. And the moon, like a maiden's gentle smile, lit up the heavens, while a rain of sweet-scented flowers, filled with moisture, fell down on the earth from above.... and the leader of all reached the state of all-

CELEBRATING FESTIVALS

knowledge. When, through his Buddhahood, he had [re]cognized this fact, the earth swayed like a woman drunken with wine, the sky shone bright... and the mighty drums of thunder resounded through the air. Pleasant breezes blew softly, rain fell from a cloudless sky, flowers and fruits dropped from the trees out of season – in an effort, as it were, to show reverence for him. Mandarava flowers and lotus blossoms, and also water lilies made of gold and beryl, fell from the sky on to the ground near the Shakya sage, so that it looked like a place in the world of the gods. At that moment no one anywhere was angry, ill, or sad; no one did evil, none was proud; the world became quite quiet, as though it had reached full perfection.

(Translated by E. Conze in *Buddhist Scriptures*, Penguin 1957.)

BIRTHDAY HONOURS

In 1879 Sir Edwin Arnold (1832-1904), an English schoolmaster and journalist, published his epic poem on the life of the Buddha which he called *The Light of Asia*. He had gone to India as Principal of Deccan College in Pune and had there learned Sanskrit and studied both eastern religion and culture. He became a spokesman for east-west understanding and *The Light of Asia* is only one of his works on Indian themes. As a result of reading *The Light of Asia* the Englishman Allen Bennett went out to Sri Lanka and Burma to learn about Buddhism and became the first westerner to ordain as a Buddhist monk in Burma in 1902. Bennett is now usually known by his Pali Buddhist name, Venerable Ananda Metteya.

This following extract comes immediately after Arnold's account of the Buddha's birth. It describes the festivities which he imagined the Buddha's father organized to celebrate the birthday naming of his son. The atmosphere is similar today at festivals marking the events of the Buddha's life, or the processions (*peraheras*)

The relics of the Buddha are treated with the respect and honour that was once given to kings. Here a procession of decorated elephants includes one which carries the tooth relic of the Buddha in a miniature stupa. The stupa is normally kept in the Tooth Relic Temple at Kandy in Sri Lanka. Once a year there is a festival which lasts fifteen days, called the Kandy Perahera (procession) or the Tooth Relic Festival. The climax of this festival is a candlelit procession of dancers, drummers and elephants. Everyone enjoys themselves and people come from a long way to join in.

once a year when his tooth relic is venerated in the streets of Kandy, Sri Lanka.

> The King gave order that his town should keep
> His festival; therefore the ways were swept,
> Rose-odours sprinkled in the street, the trees
> Were hung with lamps and flags, while merry crowds
> Gaped on the sword-players and posturers,
> The jugglers, charmers, swingers, rope-walkers,
> The nautch-girls in their spangled skirts, and bells
> That chime light laughter round their restless feet;
> The masquers wrapped in skins of bear and deer,
> The tiger-tamers, wrestlers, quail-fighters,
> Beaters of drum and twanglers of the wire,
> Who made the people happy by command,
> Moreover, from afar came merchant-men,
> Bringing, on tidings of this birth, rich gifts
> In golden trays; goat-shawls, and nard, and jade.
>
> Turkises, "evening-sky" tint, woven webs —
> So fine twelve folds hide not a modest face —
> Wait-cloths sewn thick with pearls, and sandalwood;
> Homage from tribute cities; so they called
> Their Prince Savârthasiddh, "All-Prospering,"
> Briefer, Siddârtha.

(*The Light of Asia* by Sir E. Arnold, M.D. Gunasena & Co. Ltd.)

REFLECTION OF A GOLDEN BUDDHA

Wesak is a festival of light to celebrate the life of the Enlightened One. Here is an account of it by a girl named Malee. Her name means "flower".

It is now the night of the full moon of May. This is a special night (called Wesak) marking the birth, enlightenment and death of the Buddha, who lived 2500 years ago. All day people have been going to the Wat [temple] to give flowers and to burn incense and listen to the monks chanting.

On the previous day houses were cleaned and garlands of flowers hung up. Sand was brought from the riverbank and piled in heaps outside the temple. Today the clean sand is spread all over the Wat courtyard, where everybody walks with bare feet. Flags and streamers are tied to high places. Buddha statues and all the holy books are carried out into the sunshine. The women wash the statues until they gleam, and dust every page of the books.

Now it is dark and Malee and her family have returned with candles. Malee has been to the Wat [temple] once today to throw scented water on to the big Buddha statue. Now this statue has been put on a platform outside the temple with many lights shining around it. All the people of the town are here, holding oil lamps or candles. Malee thinks the little flames look like stars in the darkness. People start to move round the Buddha in a great circle. Malee holds her candle high so she can see its reflection in the shining golden Buddha.

(From *Festivals of the Buddha* by A. Bancroft R.M.E.P.)

GIVING GENEROUSLY

Dana, giving, is the first on the list of perfections and a central feature in all Buddhist life. What you give depends on what you have. The greatest gift is not necessarily a material one, for example one text points out that there are two kinds of gifts, the gift of material things and the gift of the *dharma* and the greater of these is the gift of the *dharma*. Dharma is what monks and nuns can give to lay people. In turn they could not live without the generosity of the laity. Food is offered daily to monks and nuns, and each year there is the offering of robes at the *kathina* ceremony which comes at the end of the *Vassa* or rainy season retreat.

Kathina is the Pali name for a special robe made from cloth which lay people bring to the monastery. The cloth is cut into patched shapes which are then sewn together. These are like the patched robes that the Buddha suggested his monks should wear. The robe is then presented to one of the monks as the representative of the *sangha*. Originally the robes were made from scraps of cloth the monks found or were given and which they dyed a uniform colour. Now the tradition is kept even when new bales of cloth are provided by the laity.

There are many other levels of giving too. Apart from the gift of material things and *dharma*, there is the act of giving up one's life for another living being, giving love and giving away any merit earned during periods of meditation.

SHARING GIFTS

The Buddha taught how important generosity is in a person's life. The capacity to share with others transforms the heart and mind of the giver, indeed when the laity give food to monks they thank the monks for having provided them with the opportunity of giving.

Brethren, if beings knew, as I know, the ripening of sharing gifts, they would not enjoy their use without sharing them, nor would the taint of stinginess obsess the heart and stay there. Even if it were their last bit, their last morsel of food, they would not enjoy its use without sharing it, if there were any one to receive it. But inasmuch, brethren, as beings do not know, as I know, the ripening of sharing gifts, therefore they enjoy their use without sharing them, and the taint of stinginess obsesses their heart and stays there.

(Quoted in *The World of the Buddha* by L. Stryk.)

THE GIFT OF A HARE

Before his enlightenment, Gautama Buddha is called a *bodhisattva*, or "enlightenment being". This title indicates that he is on the path which leads through six or ten perfections (which include not only generosity, but patience, truthfulness, resolution and loving kindness), to enlightenment.

This story is about Gautama Buddha in a

previous life. It comes from the collection of *Jataka* tales in the *Pali Canon*. *Jataka* means "birth", and there are over five hundred stories about the many births in animal and human form which the Buddha lived through to make the progression necessary for enlightenment.

The story describes how a hare (the Buddha) persuades his friends the jackal, the otter, and the monkey, to fast for one day and give away whatever food they might have eaten to any beggar who comes their way. When put to the test by a wise spirit disguised as a monk (Sakka), each of the animals generously offers him food they have found, except the hare, who has found nothing and so offers his own life instead:

> "You've done well coming to me", the hare told him. "Go and build a fire. When it's blazing well, give me a call and I'll come and jump into it. Tonight you can eat my roasted meat, then go on your way and do your duty as a monk."

Sakka magically caused a heap of burning coals to appear, then called the hare, who shook his coat three times to make sure that there were no tiny insects in it that might die with him. Then he freely gave his body to the flames as a gift for the monk.

The flames, however, did not so much as singe a single hair of his coat . . . . Then Sakka explained who he really was . . . . Finally, he picked up a whole mountain, squeezed its juice onto the end of his finger, and drew the sign of the hare on the face of the moon so that all the world might know for an age to come of the kindness of the wise hare.

(From *Ten Buddhist Fables*, by J. Snelling and M. Hanselaar, published by the Buddhist Publication Society, 1984.)

THE GIFT OF A ROBE

This is an account of the *Kathina* ceremony as it takes place in Britain today. It is written by a Theravada monk based at Chithurst in Sussex.

> On the day of the festival people begin arriving at the monastery early — some may have come the night before. By about 10 a.m. they are beginning to settle and the requesting of the Three Refuges and Five Precepts takes place. Most Theravadin Buddhist festivals begin like this. Around 10.30 a.m. a meal is offered to the Sangha and then everyone shares in whatever has been brought along. At about 1 p.m. it is time for the ceremonial offering of cloth and requisites. The leader announces the offering and the cloth is formally presented to two monks who have been agreed upon by the Sangha. In return they announce to the Sangha the receipt of the Kathina offering and then appoint one senior and well-respected member of the community to receive the robe once it has been made up. The unanimous agreement of the Sangha is indicated by a harmonious *sadhu* ("it is well") — no dissension during a moment of silence indicating complete accord.

(From *World Religions in Education*, SHAP and C.R.E. 1987.)

Every day lay Buddhists generously give food to monks and nuns for their main meal. Once a year at the festival of Kathina, people bring larger gifts, especially cloth for the monks' robes, and there is a big celebration.

GIVING LOVING KINDNESS AND FRIENDSHIP

Someone once asked the present Dalai Lama what his religion was. His reply was very direct: "My religion is kindness." Loving kindness (*maitri*) is the first of the four highest states of mind in Buddhism (*brahma viharas*). When loving kindness is established towards someone, you become their spiritual friend (*kalyana mitra*). At its most basic level, *maitri* is friendliness, the kindly feeling towards everything that lives around you.

The faces of Buddha images show the kind of happy peace and loving kindness that Buddhists value. These qualities overlap with those of friendliness and compassion. Monks and nuns are often seen as the living examples of these virtues and of the Buddhist greeting "may all beings be happy".

GIVING LOVING KINDNESS AND FRIENDSHIP

A BOUNDLESS HEART

The *sutra* on loving kindness in the *Pali Canon* is probably one of the most well-known parts of Buddhist scripture. Most Buddhist children learn it by heart and it is frequently recited at Buddhist gatherings. It is also the basis for a meditation practice called the *metta* practice (*metta* is the Pali form of *maitri*). In the *metta* practice thoughts of loving kindness are established in one's heart like warm rays of sunshine. They are then sent out gradually and gently to those whom you like, to mere acquaintances, to those whom you do not like and finally to all beings in all directions.

> May all beings be happy and secure; may their minds be contented.
> Whatever living beings there may be — feeble or strong, long (or tall), stout, or medium, short, small, or large, seen or unseen, those dwelling far or near, those who are born and those who are yet to be born — may all beings, without exception, be happy-minded!
> Let not one deceive another nor despise any person whatever in any place. In anger or illwill let not one wish any harm to another.
> Just as a mother would protect her only child even at the risk of her own life, even so let one cultivate a boundless heart towards all beings.
> Let one's thoughts of boundless love pervade the whole world — above, below and across — without any obstruction, without any hatred, without any enmity.
> (Translated by W. Rahula in *What the Buddha Taught*, Gordon Fraser 1954.)

TRUE FRIENDSHIP

Maitri can be translated as both loving kindness and friendliness. Most of us learn about these qualities first of all in our families. The *metta sutra* uses the example of a mother's care for her child as a model for this kind of love. But it is also the most important part of the relationships we make for ourselves outside the family: our friendships. Dharmachari Subhuti is a member of the Western Buddhist Order, a new Buddhist movement founded in Britain in 1967 by the British Buddhist, the Venerable Sangharakshita. Proper friendship, Dharmachari Subhuti writes, is very unselfish and encourages us to care for more and more people. This order has a special title, that of *Kalyana Mitra* or "spiritual friend".

> True friendship is not need-based, includes no emotional dependence, and is characterized by mutual awareness. Powerful though feelings of friendship can be, they are never exclusive. If someone befriends our friend we would not feel the intense jealousy which arises so frequently in romantic love. Genuine friendliness has, in fact, a natural tendency to expand and to encompass more and more people. Deep friendship can only blossom where there is time to get to know each other; we cannot therefore become friends with everyone; time does not permit this. However, friendliness is always willing to expand to include more people.
> Real friendship involves an awareness of the other's potential. We do not simply see what they are but what they could be. Not only do we have powerful feelings of well-wishing towards our friends, but we hope that they will grow. Our friendliness would lead us to do everything we could to help them realise their potentiality. Real friendship is not need-based but growth-based and becomes fully possible when both friends are committed to developing as individuals.
> (From *Buddhism for Today* by D. Subhuti.)

SHOWING THAT YOU CARE

This is a poem from a children's magazine called *Rainbows* which is published for parents and children four times a year from the Theravada Buddhist centre at Amaravati near Hemel Hempstead. It shows how kindness can be extended to trees and animals as well as people.

Treat creatures kindly

We should treat creatures kindly
Because they're just like us
Insects may look ugly
And bees may buzz

But they don't harm us
As long as we don't harm them
We have our own houses
They have their own den.

When we climb trees
We must be sure
That we don't damage it too much
Or else it'll be raw
So if we are not careful
Things might become rare
So please treat things kindly
To show that you care.

Nicola Howard

(From *Rainbows*, December 1986.)

BEING A PART OF THE WORLD

The Buddhist greeting expresses the wish that all beings, not just human beings, be happy and secure and there is a strong sense in Buddhism of the unity of all life. We are a part of nature and not its master, so it is appropriate to care for the environment, for trees and animals as well as human beings, and to see the needs and hurts of all living things as part of our own life. The following quotation from the Pali *Dharmapada* (verse 270) puts this in a nutshell.

> A man is not noble because he injures living creatures.
> He is called noble because he does not injure living creatures.

KNOWING WHO I AM

Respecting the separateness of other living beings is one level of development. A deeper level is the appreciation of the oneness, the total unity of all life. This deeper level of development involves the capacity to feel the joys and sufferings of others as though they were our own. The Vietnamese Zen poet Thich Nhat Hanh (born in 1916) expresses this feeling in an extract from the poem *Please Call Me By My True Names*, using a series of pairs of opposites.

> I am the mayfly metamorphosing on the surface of the river,
> and I am the bird which, when spring comes, arrives in time to eat the mayfly.
>
> I am a frog swimming happily in the clear water of a pond,
> and I am the grass-snake who, approaching in silence, feeds itself on the frog.
>
> I am the child in Uganda, all skin and bones, my legs as thin as bamboo sticks,
> and I am the arms merchant, selling deadly weapons to Uganda.
>
> I am the twelve year-old girl, refugee on a small boat,
> who throws herself into the ocean after being raped by a sea pirate,
> and I am the pirate, my heart not yet capable of seeing and loving.
>
> I am a member of the politburo, with plenty of power in my hands,
> and I am the man who has to pay his "debt of blood" to my people,
> dying slowly in a forced labour camp.
>
> My joy is like spring, so warm it makes flowers bloom in all walks of life.
> My pain is like a river of tears, so full it fills all four oceans.
>
> Please call me by my true names, so I can hear all my cries and laughs at once,
> so I can see that my joy and pain are one.
>
> Please call me by my true names, so I can wake up and so the door of my heart can be left open, the door of compassion.

(*Please call me by my true names* by Thich Nhat Hanh, published by the Buddhist Peace Fellowship.)

RESPECT AND ECONOMICS

The distinguished twentieth-century economist, Ernst Schumacher, wrote a chapter in *Small is Beautiful* on Buddhist Economics in which he contrasts the prevailing modern economic attitudes with traditional Buddhist values. Modern attitudes involve complex life-styles and a harsh and improvident treatment of those things upon which we depend, such as water and trees. Buddhists advocate simplicity and harmonious co-operation with nature as its child not its tyrant ruler.

The teaching of the Buddha, on the other hand, enjoys a reverent and non-violent attitude not only to all sentient beings but also, with great emphasis, to trees. Every follower of the Buddha ought to plant a tree every few years and look after it until it is safely established, and the Buddhist economist can demonstrate without difficulty that the universal observation of this rule would result in a high rate of genuine economic development independent of any foreign aid. Much of the economic decay of south-east Asia (as of many other parts of the world) is undoubtedly due to a heedless and shameful neglect of trees.

(From *Small is Beautiful*, by E. Schumacher, Sphere/Abacus 1974.)

ENGAGED AND PRACTICAL

There are many areas of life that involve such big questions about pain, suffering, failure, insecurity and bereavement that it is often a temptation to avoid them, pretending that the issues or the people are not there, or that we will not face them until we have to. The danger of these attitudes, as well as the positive need for compassion, leads many Buddhists to active involvement in practical groups like the following.

Buddhist Animal Rights Group
The Buddhist Animal Rights Group aims to get Buddhists and Animal Liberation workers active in non-violent knowledgeable protests with the object of freeing all animals from human induced suffering.

The Buddhist Peace Fellowship
The Buddhist Peace Fellowship aims to make clear public witness to the Buddha Way as a way of peace and protection of all beings; to raise peace and ecological concerns among Buddhists; to work to end the persecution of Buddhists and Buddhism.

The Buddhist Hospice Project
The aims of the Project are to provide physical care, emotional support and spiritual counselling, from a Buddhist philosophical/psychological perspective, for dying people and their relatives; and to work closely with the hospice movement where possible.

(Given in *The Buddhist Directory* from The Buddhist Society, 58, Eccleston Sq., London.)

Mindfulness can be a part of every activity in a person's life. A lot can be learned from raking up leaves and thinking about the cycle of nature which is illustrated in the life-cycle of a tree. Here a Buddhist nun rakes up the leaves that have fallen in the autumn. The leaves can be used for compost to nourish the soil and in Japanese Zen monasteries the raked leaves are often used to heat water for baths.

DEVELOPING COMPASSION

Some Buddhists would say that the essence of Buddhism is compassion. It is from compassion that Gautama Buddha taught others the path and it is the compassionate heart that involves itself in helping all beings to their fulfilment in enlightenment, whatever the cost to itself. This is particularly important in the *bodhisattva* ideal, for those who take a vow to postpone their own entry into Nirvana to help others.

MEDITATION ON COMPASSION

This is from a meditation text written by the Indian Buddhist master Kamalasila in the eighth century CE. It is a standard guidebook for Mahayana Buddhists particularly, and takes up themes developed elsewhere, such as the gradual sending of thoughts of loving kindness and compassion outwards into all parts of the world.

> ... And thus he understands that the entire world is licked by the blazing flames of suffering; and he meditates upon compassion for all beings, for he knows that they abhor their pain as he does his own.
>
> He meditates first, then, upon those whom he loves: he sees how they must bear the many sufferings we have described; they are all the same as he, and he sees no difference among them.
>
> Then he meditates upon those to whom he is neutral: he considers that in the beginningless world there is no being who has not been his kinsman a hundred times, and he awakens compassion for them as for those he loves.
>
> Then he meditates upon his enemies also, and he realizes that they are all the same as he is, and he awakens compassion for his enemies even as for those he loves.
>
> And thus gradually he meditates upon all beings in the ten directions: he awakens his compassion for all beings equally, that they are as dear to him as his own suffering children, that they are his own family, and he wishes to lead them out of pain. Then is his compassion made perfect, and it is called great compassion ....

(From *The Buddhist Experience* by S. Beyer.)

THE WAY OF THE BODHISATTVA

Another eighth-century Buddhist called Shantideva, who was a master at the monastic university at Nalanda in India, here describes the main features of the *bodhisattva's* approach to life.

> May all who say bad things to me
> Or cause me any other harm,
> And those who mock and insult me
> Have the fortune to fully awaken.
>
> May I be a protector for those without one,
> A guide for all travellers along the way;
> May I be a bridge, a boat and a ship
> For all who wish to cross the water.
>
> May I be an island for those who seek one

DEVELOPING COMPASSION

Buddhist monks and nuns are normally very strict about their relationships with members of the opposite sex and they do not normally stand chatting in the street. However, if people are poor and in trouble, or need help and encouragement, then this is more important than rules, and monks like this one in Thailand are happy to help.

And a lamp for those desiring light,
May I be a bed for those who wish to rest
And a slave for all who want a slave.

Likewise for the sake of all that lives
Do I give birth to an Awakening Mind,
And likewise shall I too
Successively follow the practices.

May the naked find clothing,
The hungry find food;
May the thirsty find water
And delicious drinks.

May the poor find wealth,
Those weak with sorrow find joy;
May the forlorn find new hope,
Constant happiness and prosperity.

May all who are sick and ill
Quickly be freed from their illness,
And may every disease in the world
Never occur again.

May the frightened cease to be afraid
And those bound be freed;
May the powerless find power,
And may people think of benefiting one another.

May all the pains of living creatures
Ripen solely upon myself,
And through the power of the community of enlightened ones
May all beings experience happiness.

(A *Guide to the Bodhisattva's Way of Life* translated by S. Batchelor, Library of Tibetan Works & Archives 1979.)

LOVE WITHOUT DESIRE OR EXPECTATION

On his journey in Ladakh, Andrew Harvey met and talked to a Swiss Buddhist who was visiting Ladakh from his Tibetan Buddhist monastery in Switzerland. He told Harvey a traditional Buddhist tale about compassion.

"Do you know the story of the Buddha and the prostitute? It is the story that moves me most, I think, of any that I know. When he was young, the Buddha was considered very handsome. Some of his enemies wanted to discredit him, and so they sent to see him the most famous courtesan of his time. The Buddha liked her and they spoke of many things. She was very beautiful and witty. She offered herself to him. The Buddha smiled at her and said, "I will love you when no one else loves you; I will love you when every other love has abandoned you." At this, she grew very angry and left him. Almost forty years later, the Buddha was dying and being carried to his final resting-place on a wooden bier. He saw a figure huddled in rags in the shadow of a wall. It was a leper, a woman, an old hunchback with half her face eaten away. The Buddha dismounted from his bier, and walked across the waste between him and the woman and folded her quietly in his arms."

(From *Journey in Ladakh*, by A. Harvey, Flamingo 1984.)

GIVING EVERYTHING YOU HAVE

Gautama Buddha taught people that it is only when you are on firm ground yourself that you can help someone stuck in the mud. This is why purifying the mind and heart through meditation is so important for a Buddhist. The Theravada and Mahayana scriptures are full of stories of those who are able to give themselves in some way for the happiness and welfare of other beings. This can be through teaching them, caring for them when they are ill, or even giving your life for them.

THE HUNGRY TIGRESS

In order to become an enlightened being Gautama Buddha, like any other being on that path, had to progress through many lives in many realms. In these lives he learnt the perfections of attitudes and behaviour that are mentioned elsewhere in this book. These include generosity, patience, truthfulness and loving kindness and are called the *paramitas* or perfections. These are all illustrated in the stories of his previous births called the *Jataka* tales. Buddhists tell them a lot to their children. In this one the Buddha appears in the form of Prince Mahasattva who gave his life for a hungry tigress.

The tale describes how three princes, while out walking in a beautiful park, come upon a tigress dying from exhaustion and starvation, surrounded by her new-born cubs. Each of the princes expresses his feelings of distress and pity for the unfortunate tigress, but say "who would sacrifice himself to preserve her life?" However Prince Mahasattva says:

"It is difficult for people like us, who are so fond of our lives and bodies, and who have so little intelligence. It is not at all difficult, however, for others, who are true men, intent on benefiting their fellow-creatures, and who long to sacrifice themselves. Holy men are born of pity and compassion."

As he himself possesses "boundless compassion" he is eager to give his very life for another:

The friendly prince then threw himself down in front of the tigress. But she did nothing to him. The Bodhisattva noticed that she was too weak to move. As a merciful man he had no sword with him. He therefore cut his throat with a sharp piece of bamboo, and fell down near the tigress. She noticed the Bodhisattva's body all covered with blood, and in no time ate up all the flesh and blood, leaving only the bones.
(From *Buddhist Scriptures* by E. Conze, published by Penguin.)

A GIFT OF LOVE IS NEVER LITTLE

This story from China emphasizes that it is the intention behind giving a gift that counts. Gifts must also be received with kindness.

A young priest is collecting gold and silver from a rich merchant's household, to help make a great statue of the Buddha. Ya-teo, a little slave-girl, offers him a little copper coin, precious to her because it is her only possession:

> He asked for their gifts and everyone gave willingly. The ladies of the household gave gold and silver ornaments, rings, combs and bracelets. The master of the house gave precious vessels and gold and silver money; the servants gave silver and copper coins, and Ya-teo said happily to herself, "I can give too!" She held out her precious coin to the priest and said, "It is mine to give. I found it when I swept the yard".
>
> Instead of taking it, the young priest shook his head as if he disliked it. "Should I put a dirty copper coin with that for the image of Lord Buddha?" he said pointing to the shining heap of treasure that lay before him. And he gathered it up and went away to the temple of Lin-Hsien without another word to Ya-teo.
>
> The young priest went proudly back with his precious load. Other priests came also, bringing more and more treasure and soon all that was needed had been gathered together. Then the metal for the statue was melted and poured into the mould and set to cool, but when the mould was taken away, it was seen that the statue was marked with ugly lines and patches. "The metal is badly mixed", said the priests and they melted it again, more carefully still. Once more it was poured into the mould but this time too it was spoiled.
>
> Then the head priest called the priests together and asked about the gifts they had brought. "Was all done in love and kindness?" he asked. "For only love must go to the making of the image of him who taught us of love."
>
> When it came to the turn of the young priest, he confessed how he had refused the dirty coin offered by the little slave-girl.
>
> "My son", said the priest, "that was not well done. She loved and gave all she had; none could do more. There can be no greater gift. Now do as I tell you. Return and humbly accept it, for there is need of Ya-teo's gift." So the young priest went back to the house of Liu-Teh-Jong and to Ya-teo's great surprise, she was sent for and told that he had come to ask humbly for the treasure which she had offered and which he had refused. She gave it joyfully.
>
> The priest returned and once more the metal was melted and poured into the mould and last of all the coin was dropped in also. When the mould was taken away, there stood the great statue — fair, smiling and perfect. On its breast, just over the heart, was the copper coin, Ya-teo's gift, no longer dull and dirty but fair and smiling too!

(From *Religion in the Multi-Faith School*, ed. O. Cole, Stanley Thornes 1983.)

A SACRIFICE BY FIRE

In 1963, during the Vietnamese war, there were pictures in the western press of Buddhist monks setting themselves on fire in the streets and dying while sitting in meditation. In June 1965, a Vietnamese Zen monk who is now active in the Buddhist Peace movement, wrote to Dr Martin Luther King to try to explain these burnings. Here is an extract from his letter:

> To burn oneself by fire is to prove that what one is saying is of the utmost importance. There is nothing more painful than burning oneself. To say something while experiencing this kind of pain is to say it with utmost courage, frankness, determination and sincerity. . . .
>
> I believe with all my heart that the monks who burned themselves did not aim at the death of the oppressors but only at a change in their policy. Their enemies are not man. They are intolerance, fanaticism, dictatorship, cupidity, hatred and discrimination which lie within the heart of man. I also believe with all my being that

GIVING EVERYTHING YOU HAVE

the struggle for equality and freedom you lead in Birmingham, Alabama, is not really aimed at the whites but only at intolerance, hatred and discrimination. These are the real enemies of man — not man himself. In our unfortunate fatherland we are trying to plead desperately: do not kill man, even in man's name. Please kill the real enemies of man which are present everywhere, in our very hearts and minds.
(Vietnam: The Lotus in a Sea of Fire by Thich Nhat Hanh, S.C.M. 1967.)

Body language says a great deal. These Tibetan pilgrims have made considerable sacrifices and come a long way to visit Bodh Gaya, the place where the Buddha was enlightened. They show their complete devotion to his teaching by going round the sacred sites in a series of prostrations right down to the ground. The prostrations not only show their attitude of complete self-sacrifice, but also help to develop humility in the body, speech and mind of the person.

GOING ON A PILGRIMAGE

There are many different reasons why people go on pilgrimages. Curiosity about history might draw you to N.E. India, where you can walk in the footsteps of Gautama Buddha by visiting the four main sites connected with his life. Buddhist history and culture come to life in places such as Borobudur in Java, or the Shwe Dagon Pagoda in Rangoon in Burma. The effort to climb overnight to the top of a mountain such as Sri Pada (also called Adam's Peak) in Sri Lanka brings the reward of magnificent views as the sun rises. In Britain, Buddhists often drive long distances to visit a Dharma Centre, meet other Buddhists and hear teachings. None of these pilgrimages is obligatory, but all of them can bring a sense of fellowship with other Buddhists and a deeper understanding of the religious tradition.

WITH FEELINGS OF REVERENCE

The *sutra* which describes the death of Gautama Buddha records his suggestion that his followers should visit four places linked with his life.

> There are four places, Ananda, which the devoted person should visit with feelings of reverence. What are the four?
> The place, Ananda, at which the devoted person can say: "Here the Buddha was born!" is a spot to be visited with feelings of reverence.
> The place, Ananda, at which the devoted person can say: "Here, the Buddha attained to supreme and highest wisdom!" is a spot to be visited with feelings of reverence.
> The place, Ananda, at which the devoted person can say: "Here the Wheel of the Dharma was set in motion by the Buddha!" is a spot to be visited with feelings of reverence.
> The place, Ananda, at which the devoted person can say: "Here the Buddha passed finally away . . ." is a spot to be visited with feelings of reverence.

(Adapted from the Mahaparinirvana Sutra, in *The Buddha's Philosophy of Man* by T. Ling, Dent 1981.)

PILGRIMS TOGETHER

Japan has many pilgrim sites linked with famous holy men in the history of Japanese Buddhism. One of the most famous is an ancient circular route round 88 sacred places on the island of Shikoku. The places are associated with the saint Kukai, or Kobo Daishi (774-835 CE) and pilgrims who walk the route dress like him and recall the stories of his life as they go round. They feel so close to him that they say: "We two-pilgrims together."

At the first temple pilgrims are given a traditional leaflet which is a mixture of practical and spiritual advice. It carries the warnings that pilgrims can be exploited on the journey as well as helped in their faith. It ends with the phrase constantly used by pilgrims at this site: *Namu*

GOING ON A PILGRIMAGE

Daishi Henjo Kongo, which could be translated as "Homage to Kobo Daishi, who impels our quest, who guides and accompanies us."

The pilgrim is not to veil his body in impurity or harbour evil thoughts in his soul; he should enter upon the ... journey with a cleansed body and a pure heart. In whatever difficulties and disagreeable situations he may find himself, he should let no thought of anger rise in him. ...

Those who set out together should assist one another lovingly and obligingly. If they meet a weak pilgrim or one troubled by illness, they should spend themselves in caring for him; that is charity after the Buddha's heart. In the choice of companions met along the way one must be cautious; one must consider that there are times when it is pleasant to have a comrade to talk with, but there are also occasions when one's faith in a companion is betrayed. For there are bad people who have the most honest appearance; they approach and pretend that they want to point out a shorter way, to deliver efficacious prayers, or to teach a secret magic; they end by forcibly taking money or even violating women. Such people are to be found here and there upon the roads of Shikoku: those who wear pilgrim garb to hunt for their livelihood. ...

A hasty journey with a heart full of business does not lead to piety. One is only brought to shame by it. Without other intention or thought, calmly and without haste, with "Namu Daishi Henjo Kongo" upon one's lips — that is how to make the true pilgrimage.

Namu Daishi Henjo Kongo.

(From a Buddhist pilgrim leaflet (translated by Oliver Statler) in *Japanese Pilgrimage*, Pan Books 1984.)

The daunting height of Adam's Peak or Sri Pada in Sri Lanka says something about the nature of pilgrimage. The goal is often far away and a great effort has to be made to get there. It is this effort which makes a pilgrimage an act of great merit. All kinds of qualities such as hope and endurance are developed in the struggles of the journey. These are then applied to the journey of life.

FINDING PEACE

A physical journey becomes a spiritual pilgrimage when it is made with the right intention. It is possible to be on a spiritual journey just by practising your religion and not travelling anywhere outside yourself. In this way both meditation and the journey of life are pilgrimages. The following three Buddhists undertake different kinds of pilgrimages.

1. For us, a pilgrimage is to hear a lecture – as a pilgrimage: to hear the Dalai Lama, to hear some eminent Buddhist scholar. It's not just listening to a lecture, but a pilgrimage, because in Buddhism we talk all the time about the transmission of the *dharma*: and the transmission for us is not just a talking, or a communication, but almost a literal, physical, passing across . . . it is a physical feeling of vitality that you get when you go to someone who has gone very far along the path. It is a finding and a being found.

2. When I was even a boy, we were taken to Nepal, where Lord Buddha was born. Near Nepal, there are two very high temples, Bhalyoulchoten and Phapashingon. I don't know when they were constructed, I can't remember; but they are very famous. So we go there for the pilgrimage, and we go there with full conviction, with no money – we just go very simply. When I was there, I felt that I've got to do a little bit more: I've got to do more. "Yes," I felt, "this is worth doing, this is something good happening: I must do a little bit more." Then it teaches me that always, when something good is happening, it tells that I've got to do a little bit more.

3. I went to *Sripada*, the Footprint of the Buddha, only about seven or eight months ago, and the feeling I have is complete peace, and as if nothing can harm you. And you are there, and the whole place is filled with peace and love, and loving kindness, that kind of thing. And I feel, What am I doing as a person? I should be trying – I mean this is my own feeling: I think, Oh well, I must do something to eradicate poverty in the world: I must do something worth while. I am here now, and I'll be just gone the next day and I have not fulfilled what I should do, or I have not made use of my opportunities that I have had. And then the same thing I experienced at Radipura, which is the ancient capital of Sri Lanka, where there is a statue of Buddha, the *Samadhi* statue, of the time when he was meditating; and I think it's Pandit Nehru who came there when he was Prime Minister of India: whenever he used to come to Sri Lanka, he used to always, evidently, come and stand in front of the statue; because he said that gave him absolute peace for the time when he was there. I have quite often stood in front of that statue, and I think to myself, Well, this is complete peace; and you are quite oblivious of everything else, the whole world as such. And this is complete peace.

(From *Worlds of Faith*, by J. Bowker, BBC Enterprises 1983.)

ACCEPTING DEATH

Buddhists try to remember that life will come to an end for all of us. This helps to keep things in perspective and is perhaps especially important when we are young and bursting with health. One of the four signs which made Gautama search for enlightenment was the sight of a funeral procession. Kisagotami's waking up to the *dharma* came through understanding death (see page 8). When flowers are put in a shrine room the words that are spoken remind us of both their beauty and of impermanence.

Anitya (impermanence), is one of the three marks of existence taught by Buddhists. The other two are closely linked to it. *Duhkha* describes the sense of unsatisfactoriness or suffering that is experienced as material possessions break or are destroyed, as our relationships constantly change and when we lose those we love through old age, sickness and death. Individuals, too, are constantly changing and *anatman* (not-self) expresses the idea that we have no eternal essence that separates us from all other forms of life. The wisest among us learn to live as selfless persons.

LIKE A FLOWER

There are many sayings in the Buddhist scriptures about impermanence and death. The following are from the teachings in the *Pali Canon* of Gautama Buddha (see illustration on the next page).

Death carries off a man who is gathering life's flowers whose mind is distracted, even as a flood carries off a sleeping village.

All created things are impermanent, when one by wisdom realizes [this], he heeds not [this world of] sorrow.
(The *Dharmapada* translated by S. Radhakrishnan Oxford University Press.)

UNDERSTANDING THE SIGNS

The *Diamond* or *Thunderbolt Sutra* is a Mahayana text which dates from about the fourth century CE. Its name comes from the word *vajra* (meaning diamond or thunderbolt), describing something which is indestructible and can cut through anything. The Diamond Sutra cuts through confusion to show Buddhists the truth about the way things are. In this extract, a variety of images of impermanence are used to demonstrate the nature of life.

As stars, a fault of vision, as a lamp,
A mockshow, dew drops, or a bubble,
A dream, a lightening flash, or cloud,
So one should view what is conditioned.
(The *Diamond Sutra* translated by E. Conze in *Buddhist Wisdom Books* George Allen & Unwin 1953.)

ACCEPTING DEATH

The huge images of the Buddha reclining peacefully on his death bed usually make a considerable impression on anyone who sees them. Accounts of his death describe how the Buddha lay down calmly between two sala trees, whose blossoms then cascaded onto his body.

Buddhists are encouraged to make every effort so that their own progress towards dying and Nirvana has the same qualities of serenity and acceptance that can be seen in these images.

SOFTLY CHANTING

Death is an important rite of passage in Buddhism (see the next chapter) in a way that marriage, for instance, has not traditionally been in Buddhist cultures. At a funeral monks chant special verses from the scriptures. These will help to make merit and also remind the mourners of the meaning of death. Here, a western writer reflects on the different attitudes to death in Thailand while she is living there and learning Buddhist meditation.

The feeling that I often sensed amongst Buddhist mourners almost defied definition. Death to them seems to exact no pity, no rebellion, no mournful wailings, nor does it promote exultations or rejoicings. Death brings with it a mood, fragile and tender.

The mourners reveal these qualities, yet death somehow does not command the importance, the finality that it does to Westerners....

ACCEPTING DEATH

The Oriental views himself and the world differently. He views death and dying with less pure physical fear because he believes that there are many more lives to live....

Buddhist teachings focus on life — since life and death are one. Death (or changing) is only a part of life. Of course there are rites and rituals attached to the cremation or burial of a Buddhist and the families reflect sadness. But because the Theravada Buddhist believes that he has many lives to live — hundreds, perhaps, hundreds of thousands yet to come — there is an absence of finality in the cessation of one. For the Buddhist, death is not a trauma, but more the continuation of a continuous process of changing, decaying and arising that somehow lies outside the notion of death as a finality.

The essence of this understanding of death is softly chanted by monks at funerals — "All things in *samsara* (the world of life and death) are impermanent. To be happy there can be no clinging."

(From A *Meditator's Diary*, by J. Hamilton-Merritt Souvenir Press 1979.)

CREMATING AND REMEMBERING

Buddhists usually cremate the body of a dead person although some Buddhists do bury their dead. In Tibet, where wood is very scarce, bodies are exposed to the elements and given a "sky burial". B*hikshus* (monks) are involved both at funerals and in later ceremonies for remembering the dead. These are different from the rituals linked with marriage (see page 25) where it is only in recent times that monks have had an active role to play.

Monks use the occasion of a funeral to teach about the impermanence of life and to express the hope that all beings will eventually attain the happy state of Nirvana. This wish is often printed on the announcements of a death as well as circulated on printed pieces of paper at the time of the funeral. Relatives also remember the dead and their progress in rebirth towards Nirvana with various acts of *dana* (generosity or giving) to *bhikshus*, which make merit. There are often ceremonies after seven days, three months and annually on the anniversary of the death. Water-pouring rites are also linked with the idea of making merit which can be shared by the dead.

When the person who has died is a Buddha (enlightened one) or an *arhant* (saint) or an especially great teacher, relics are collected after the cremation. These may be placed in a *stupa* (burial mound) or in a B*uddha-rupa* (image of the Buddha). Whenever the Buddhist sees a *stupa* in the countryside or a B*uddha-rupa* in a shrine room it is a reminder of the *dharma* (teaching) and it is honoured because of that.

These Buddhists monks in Thailand are on their way to a funeral. As they go, they exchange greetings with lay people and are generally cheerful, as Buddhists are encouraged to be in the face of death. They are carrying pieces of paper inserted into prayer sticks. On them are texts about the impermanence of life and the wish that all beings may happily attain Nirvana. Monks usually speak about these themes and distribute the texts at the funeral service.

CREMATING AND REMEMBERING

GRIEF WITH GARLANDS

The monks who were close followers of Gautama Buddha gave his body to the lay people in the nearest town, the Mallas of Kusinara, to arrange the cremation. The *sutra* from the *Pali Canon* which describes the arrangements shows the tension between sadness at someone's death and making the appropriate celebrations. The venerable Ananda was one of the Buddha's closest followers.

> But the venerable Ananda went to the council hall of the Mallas of Kusinara; and when he had arrived there he informed them, saying: "The Blessed One .... is dead; do, then, whatever seemeth to you fit."
>
> And when they had heard this saying of the venerable Ananda, the Mallas, with their young men and their maidens and their wives were grieved, and sad, and afflicted at heart. And some of them wept, dishevelling their hair; and some stretched forth their arms and wept, and some fell prostrate on the ground, and some reeled to and fro in anguish at the thought: "Too soon has the Exalted One died! Too soon has the Happy One passed away! Too soon has the light gone out of the world!"
>
> Then the Mallas of Kusinara gave orders to their attendants, saying: "Gather together perfumes and garlands, and all the music in Kusinara!"
>
> And the Mallas of Kusinara took perfumes and garlands, and all the musical instruments, and five hundred suits of apparel and went to where the body of the Exalted One lay. There they passed the day in paying honour, reverence, respect and homage to the remains of the Exalted One with dancing, and hymns and music and with garlands and perfumes ....
>
> Then the Mallas of Kusinara said to the venerable Ananda: "What should be done, Lord, with the remains of the [Buddha]? As men treat the remains of a King of Kings, so should they treat the remains of a [Buddha]."...
>
> They wrap the body in a new cloth. When that is done, they wrap it in carved cotton wool. When that is done they wrap it in a new cloth — and so on ... then they place the body in an oil vessel of iron, and cover that close with another oil vessel of iron. Then they build a funeral pyre of all kinds of perfumes, and burn the body ... and then at the four crossroads they erect a stupa ... and whoever shall there place garlands or perfumes or paint, or make salutation there, or become in its presence calm in heart — that shall long be to

(The *Mahaparinirvana sutra* translated by Rhys Davids, Pali Text Society 1966.)

GIVING GIFTS FOR DEPARTED ONES

In Theravada Buddhist countries such as Sri Lanka, the ceremonies at a funeral and on the anniversaries of a person's death usually involve giving food and cloth for robes to monks. All of these make merit for the relatives which they hope will be shared by those who have died. This shows how family and friends care about the dead. Buddhists know, however, that they cannot alter someone's *Karma* (deeds, based on intention which affect their rebirth) and that there is no entity called a "soul" or a person to whom they can now relate in some way. During the ceremonies the monks may quote verses from poems such as the following from a book in the *Pali Canon* called "The *Sutra* of behaviour due to relatives":

As river beds when full can bear
The water down to fill the sea,
So giving given here can serve
The ghosts of the departed kin.

"He gave to me, he worked for me,
He was my kin, friend, intimate."
Give gifts, then, for departed ones,
Recalling what they used to do.

No weeping, nor yet sorrowing,
Nor any kinds of mourning, aids
Departed Ones, whose kin remain
(Unhelpful to them acting) thus.

But when this offering is given
Well placed in the community
For them, then it can serve them long
In future and at once as well.

The True Idea for relatives has thus been shown
And how high honour to departed ones is done,
And how the *bhikshus* can be given strength as well
And how great merit can be stored away by you.

(From *Minor Readings* translated by Bhikkhu Nanamoli, Pali Text Society, 1978.)

THE POWER TO INSPIRE

Here is a modern Buddhist account of the cremation of a Tibetan teacher Choqyam Triungpa Rimpoche. He came to the West in 1963 and taught in Canada during the last years of his life. The account is written by Michael Hookham, a westerner who has been a Buddhist for over 30 years.

> The cremation was conducted in public on slightly raised ground amidst the open countryside, hills and woods of Vermont. Although considered a sacred place because of the nature of the event itself, there was no attempt to separate the cremation place from the surrounding countryside, again contrasting strongly with the Western notion of an enclosed private crematorium surrounded by a "garden of rest" . . . .
>
> Unlike cremation in the West the temperature of the fire is deliberately kept sufficiently low so as to ensure that some of the bones will remain after the fire has cooled (these will generally be the larger bones and fragments of the smaller bones). The next day the ashes were searched for bones which were then removed prior to being placed in a special *stupa* . . . . The ashes were then also removed and taken to a meditation room where Rimpoche's students searched for smaller bones and prepared the ashes for incorporation into any smaller *stupas* made of clay . . . .

All the events I have described affected me deeply and their significance for me is not readily communicable. Perhaps I can express it to some degree by saying that because of actual involvement with all the stages of Rimpoche's death his power to inspire one in the quest for the discovery of the awakened mind is experienced as a paradox: the essence of the teacher is not his physical manifestation, but neither is it apart from it.

("Death and Continuity" by Michael Hookham in *Human Potential* Autumn 1987 Vol II No 3.)

ENTERING INTO NIRVANA

Buddhists have confidence that, after countless births, all beings will become enlightened and enter into the eternal state called in Sanskrit Nirvana. This is the proper destiny of living beings, all of whom have the Buddha Nature within them, hidden like the moon behind the clouds. Beings who are already well on the way to enlightenment work selflessly, compassionately and skilfully to help others to Nirvana with them.

Nirvana is the blowing out of the flames of all greed, hatred and ignorance (the three fires which fuel the flames of *samsara*). It is a state beyond suffering, impermanence and not-self – the three marks of existence (see page 53). It includes all the qualities of peace and true happiness experienced only fragmentarily here in *samsara*. But it is almost impossible to give any adequate description of it.

Just as it is impossible to describe Nirvana in words, so it is impossible to picture it. The circle is a universal symbol of eternity and perfection and an empty circle, like this one painted by a Zen master, shows that at Nirvana the wheel of samsara is completely emptied of greed, hatred and ignorance. It stands out like the disc of the full moon when all the clouds are blown away.

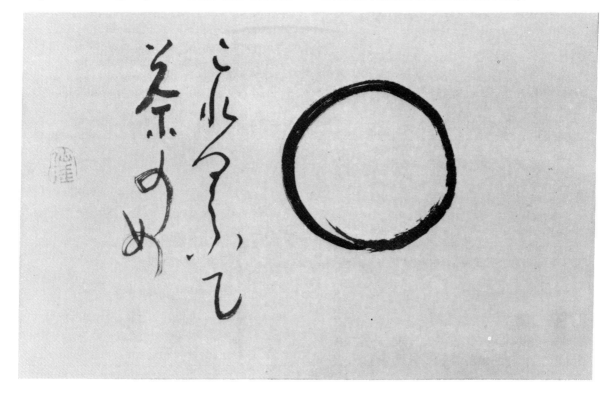

BEYOND THE POWER OF WORDS

Buddhists believe that it is dangerous to think that purely human words can describe the ultimate state of Nirvana. So a range of terms are used. Enlightenment can be seen as inward, the Buddha Nature which is in all beings. It is also called "Suchness" or "Thatness": the true nature of all that is. The following quotation is from the *Pali Canon*. In it Gautama Buddha attempts to explore what Nirvana is with some of his followers. He has to use a lot of negatives and contradictions to show that it is unlike most of our experience here and is "beyond the power of words".

> Monks, there is that sphere wherein is neither earth nor water, fire nor air; it is not the infinity of space, nor the infinity of perception; it is not nothingness, nor is it neither idea nor non-idea; it is neither this world nor the next, nor is it both; it is neither the sun nor the moon.
>
> Monks, I say it neither comes nor goes, it neither abides nor passes away; it is not caused, established, begun, supported; it is the end of suffering.

What I call the selfless is hard to see, for it is not easy to see the truth. But he who knows it penetrates his craving; and for him who sees it, there is nothing there.

Monks, there is an unborn, unbecome, unmade, unconditioned. Monks, if there were not an unborn, unbecome, unmade, unconditioned, then we could not here know any escape from the born, become, made, conditioned.

But since there is an unborn, unbecome, unmade, unconditioned, then we know there is an escape from the born, become, made, conditioned.

For the attached there is wandering, but for the unattached there is no wandering; without wandering there is serenity; where there is serenity there is no lust; without lust there is neither coming nor going; without coming or going there is neither passing away nor being reborn; without passing away or being reborn there is neither this life nor the next, nor anything between them. It is the end of suffering.
(*Udana* (utterances) in *Khuddaka-Nikaya*, edited by Bhikkhu Kashyap, Pali Publications Board 1959.)

NIRVANA IS UNLIKE ANYTHING ELSE

"The Questions of King Milinda", or the *Milindapanha*, is a Pali text which reports conversations between a Buddhist monk, Nagasena, and the Greek King Milinda whose empire stretched into north-west India. The king is also called Menander or Menandros in Greek sources. He probably lived in the second century BCE, but the text was written down later, in about the first century CE. Milinda asks a lot of searching questions in his attempt to understand Buddhist ideas. They are still very much the standard questions people ask today and Nagasena's answers have become classics of interpretation. Nibbana is the Pali word for Nirvana.

> Great king, just as, although the great ocean exists, it is impossible to measure the water or count the living beings that make their abode there, precisely so, great king, although Nibbana really exists, it is impossible to make clear the form or figure or age or dimensions of Nibbana....
>
> Just as the lotus is not polluted by water, so also Nibbana is not polluted by any of the Depravities....

Just as water is cool and quenches fever, so also Nibbana is cool and quenches every one of the Depravities. . . .

But again further, medicine puts an end to bodily ills. Precisely so Nibbana puts an end to all sufferings. . . .

Just as food is the support of life of all human beings, so also Nibbana, once realised, is the support of life, for it destroys old age and death. . . .

Just as a mountain-peak is exceedingly lofty, so also Nibbana is exceedingly lofty.

(The *Milindapanha* from *The World of the Buddha*, edited by L. Stryk.)

THE HEART'S MESSAGE

This short extract is from a classic text of Zen Buddhism. It is called *Mu-mon-ku*, "the no gate barrier", or *The Gateless Gate*. It was put together by the Chinese master Ekai, who is also called Mumon and who lived between 1183 and 1260 CE. He recalls how he used old *koans* (problem-setting verses) to try to challenge his students into an enlightened state of mind. Passing through the gateless gate means passing beyond reason and argument into an instinctive state of awareness, as the Zen Buddhist responded when the Buddha held up a flower (see page 8).

> Words cannot describe everything
> The heart's message cannot be delved in words.
> If one receives words literally, he will be lost.
> If he tries to explain with words, he will not attain enlightenment in this life.

("The Gateless Gate" by Ekai tr. N. Senzaki & P. Reps in *Zen Flesh, Zen Bones*.)

DIFFICULT WORDS

(Words are given in their Sanskrit form, followed by the Pali form in brackets.)

abhidharma (*abhidhamma*) a further or higher layer of explanation of the teachings. The third section of the *Pali Canon* is called the Abhidharma Pitaka.

Amitabha (*Amida* in Japanese) the name of a cosmic Buddha. Those who say his name with faith are reborn in his Pure Land from where he can help them to Nirvana.

anatman (*anata*) the teaching that there is no eternal or immortal entity in beings which will not change or decay and which survives death.

anitya (*anicca*) the idea that all things are impermanent.

bhikshu (*bhikkhu*) those who live from the alms or offerings given to them by lay Buddhists. Often translated as monk.

bhikshuni (*bhikkhuni*) the feminine of the above. Usually translated as nun.

bodhisattva (*bodhisatta*) a being who is fully capable of gaining enlightenment but who puts helping others before his own entry into Nirvana.

brahma-viharas the four advanced states of mind of loving-kindness, compassion, sympathetic joy and equanimity.

buddha a title meaning an enlightened or awakened one. There are many buddhas but perhaps the most famous is Gautama (Gotama), who is also known as Shakyamuni (wise man of the Shakya clan) and Siddhartha, his personal name.

Buddha Nature a term used mainly by Mahayana Buddhists which refers to the nature of enlightenment which we all share, but which is hidden particularly by ignorance.

dana can be translated as giving or generosity. It is the opposite of greed and one of the most basic Buddhist virtues.

dharma (*dhamma*) has a wide range of meanings. These include teaching and truth.

duhkha (*dukkha*) is usually translated by the word suffering, but has the broad sense of all the imperfections of life as we know it, and the sense of unsatisfactoriness.

kalyana-mitra a spiritual friend.

karma ((*kamma*) can be translated as "deeds", but has the fuller sense of the thoughts, words and deeds that affect our future lives. It is like a seed which can produce good or bad fruit.

Mahayana "the great way", is a collective term which includes various Buddhist schools such as those in Tibet, the Pure Land and Zen schools of China and Japan. It is sometimes called Northern Buddhism.

maitri (*metta*) Loving kindness or friendliness.

Nirvana (*Nibbana*) a term for the ultimate state of being which is the goal of Buddhism. It involves the extinguishing of the fires of greed, hatred and ignorance in our lives.

Pali Canon the collection of scriptures in the Pali dialect which Theravada Buddhists believe is the closest we have to the original teachings of Gautama Buddha. It has three sections; the *Vinaya*, *Sutra* and *Abhidharma Pitakas*.

DIFFICULT WORDS

paramita there are ten qualities or perfections that lead to enlightenment in Theravada and six in Mahayana Buddhism. The ten are generosity, moral conduct, renunciation, wisdom, energetic effort, patience, truthfulness, resolution, loving kindness and equanimity.

prajna (panna) this is the opposite of ignorance and delusion and is the kind of insight, understanding and wisdom that takes beings to enlightenment.

precept Buddhists commit themselves to five, eight or ten ways of behaving which they believe will help them along the path of enlightenment.

samadhi the calm, concentrated state of meditation which is important for Buddhists. Another term which refers to the calming stage is *samatha*.

samsara the cycle of repeated birth, death and rebirth which is the state of all beings until they reach enlightenment.

sangha the assembly of the Buddhist community which is made up of four groups, male and female laity and male and female world-renouncers. The term is often used just for the world-renouncers – the monks and nuns.

sila morality or virtue, which is the first and basic stage of the path for all Buddhists. It is described in the five precepts.

stupa a burial mound built over the ashes of Gautama Buddha. These have developed different architectural styles all over the Buddhist world and may contain the relics of great saints and very old scriptures as well as those of the Buddha.

sutra (sutta) means a thread and is used for the sermons of Gautama Buddha and for any collections of teachings. One of the sections of the *Pali Canon*.

tanha the image of being thirsty is used for the state of greed or desire which is one of the three root evils in Buddhism. The other two are hatred and ignorance.

Theravada "the way of the elders" is the title for the kind of Buddhism found in places such as Sri Lanka, Burma and Thailand. It is also sometimes called Southern Buddhism or even Pali Buddhism because it uses the *Pali Canon* as its scriptures.

tripitaka (tipitaka) three baskets. A term for the *Pali Canon* which was collected in three sections.

triratna (tiratana) the three jewels or three precious things of Buddhism are the *buddha*, the *dharma* and the *sangha*. Refuge or homage to these is a part of the beginning of most Buddhist ceremonies.

upaya kausalya Buddhists believe that what and how you teach people depends on what kind of person they are. The capacity to match teaching to the person and situation is called using "skilful means". This idea of what is skilful can also be called what is appropriate.

vihara the term for a Buddhist temple or monastery. In Thailand this would be called a *wat*.

vinaya the rules of the monastic life which are collected in one of the three sections of the *Pali Canon*.

INDEX

abhidharma 4, 5, 62
America 4
Amitabha 5, 16, 62
anatman 53, 66
anitya 53, 66
arhant 56
Ashoka 4
Astasahasrika 5

bhikshu 3, 6, 31, 56, 58, 62
bhikshuni 3, 6, 62
bodhisattva 7, 27, 35, 44, 47, 62
brahma viharas 12, 26, 38, 62
buddha(s) 6, 7, 8, 10, 11, 12, 13, 14, 20, 25, 27, 30, 31, 32, 35, 44, 50, 51, 52, 54, 56, 61, 62, 63
Buddha Nature 59, 60
Buddhism 3, 6, 7, 8, 18, 24, 27, 30, 38, 43, 52, 54, 63
Burma 3, 4, 35, 50, 63

China 3, 4, 5
compassion 26, 27, 44, 46, 47

dana 31, 35, 56, 62
dharma 2, 4, 6, 7, 8, 10, 11, 15, 17, 22, 25, 32, 35, 52, 56, 63
Dharmapada 6, 10, 23, 29, 41, 53
duhkha 53, 62

Eightfold Path 6, 20
enlightenment 3, 12, 15, 18, 23, 25, 29, 31, 35, 36, 44, 53, 59, 63
Europe 4

festivals 17, 18, 32, 36
Four Noble Truths 6, 14
funeral 54, 56

Gautama 3, 4, 5, 6, 8, 10, 12, 15, 30, 31, 35, 44, 47, 50, 53, 60, 62, 63

haiku 18
Heart Sutra 5
householders 3, 6, 7

India 4, 6, 33, 44, 50

Japan 3, 4, 5, 16, 31, 50
Jataka 36, 47

kalyana mitra 38, 39
Kangyur 5
karma 57, 62
koan 61
Korea 3

lama 14
lay people 3, 7, 8, 17, 22, 23, 27, 29, 32, 35
Lotus Sutra 4, 5, 15
loving kindness 23, 26, 47 (see also *maitri*)

Mahayana 3, 4, 5, 6, 7, 14, 15, 27, 31, 44, 47, 53, 62, 63
maitri 38, 39
mantra 14
marriage 25, 54, 56
meditation 11, 14, 17, 22, 26, 27, 28, 30, 35, 44, 47, 52, 54, 58
merit 35, 54, 56, 57, 58, 62

Nichiren 4, 5, 6
Nirvana 5, 6, 7, 11, 13, 14, 15, 25, 59, 60, 61, 62, 63

Pali Canon 4, 5, 10, 12, 13, 20, 24, 27, 36, 39, 53, 57, 60, 63
paramita 5, 47, 63
pilgrimage 50, 51, 52
prajna 5, 9, 11, 63

Prajnaparamita 4, 5
precepts 17, 18, 20, 36
Pure Land 3, 4, 5, 8, 16

rebirth 5, 6, 23, 29, 57

samadhi 11, 52, 63
samsara 6, 11, 14, 55, 59, 63
sangha 4, 6, 7, 10, 11, 15, 25, 29, 32, 35, 63
Sanskrit 4, 7, 31, 33, 59, 62
sila 11, 17
Sri Lanka 3, 4, 5, 25, 32, 33, 34, 50, 51, 52, 57, 63
stupa 33, 56, 58, 63
suffering 6, 8, 11, 25, 53
Sukhavati Sutras 5
sutra 4, 5, 7, 12, 39, 50, 63

Tangyur 5
tanha 63
Thailand 3, 4, 18, 54, 56, 63
Theravada 3, 4, 5, 6, 8, 11, 14, 17, 27, 29, 31, 32, 47, 63
Tibet 3, 4, 5, 8
T'ient'ai 5
tripitaka 5
triratna 10

upaya kausalya 5, 7, 18

Vassa 32, 35
Vimalakirti Sutra 4, 5, 7, 29
Vinaya Pitaka 4, 5, 17

Wesak 33, 34
Western Buddhist Order 4, 8, 20, 22

Zen 3, 4, 7, 8, 18, 22, 30, 41, 43, 59, 61